ROSEMARY SASSOON

Keeping Chronicles

Preserving history through
written memorabilia

First published in Great Britain 2010
A&C Black Publishers
36 Soho Square
London W1D 3QY
www.acblack.com

ISBN: 978-1408-12900-5

A CIP catalogue record for this book is available from
the British Library

Page and cover design: Mike Blacker, Blacker Design
Commissioning editor: Linda Lambert
Editorial assistant: Ellen Parnavelas

This book is produced using paper that is made from
wood grown in managed, sustainable forests. It is
natural, renewable and recyclable. The logging and
manufacturing processes conform to the
environmental regulations of the country of origin.

Printed and bound in China

Contents

An indenture from 1925, letter from 1843 and a miniature of a soldier who fell at Spion Kop in the Boer War.

Introduction

The term 'Keeping Chronicles' has two meanings. It reflects the actual recording as well as the preservation of information. The object of this book is to illustrate the importance of preserving written memorabilia for several reasons; for personal satisfaction, for the future interest of the family and for the purpose of social history and further research etc.

Whereas genealogists trace the dates of their ancestors, the written trace, of itself, illuminates the character of past generations, as much as the contents of letters, diaries and other lists which chronicle their daily life. Additionally, even a childhood diary, a sketchbook or a series of letters from an interesting moment or location, may become historically significant and even suitable for publication after a very few years.

This book is organised into different categories of memorabilia from the obvious ones of letters, postcards and diaries to the less obvious ones concerning such matters as school books, day books, family cookery books, travel and other memoirs. Each chapter illustrates the different uses such memorabilia has been, or can be put to, from publication to providing clues for further research to just endless pleasure and interest. The one thing that is not dealt with anywhere in this book is the intrinsic value of written memorabilia. This is left for individuals to find out for themselves.

Delving into old letters and family documents is an emotive experience. Often, when I have given a talk on the subject or discussed this project with friends, people have produced some of their own memorabilia. Sometimes it has remained hidden in a cupboard for years, unread and neglected. I am immensely grateful to those who have allowed me to reproduce such items in this book. Then, without the expert help of designer, Michael Blacker, this intricate web of illustrations and text could never have been created.

To those specialists who have shared their expertise in the final chapter, there is a further debt of gratitude for their valuable input. This chapter looks at the subject from different angles. Together they give the reader a wider perspective into the world of museums and record offices and other archives, as well as valuable help concerning preservation and the difficult job of deciphering ancient documents.

Few households have enough storage for everything of their own, much less from their parents' homes. This is how important records and vital letters and documents are lost. The family history over a century or more can disappear in a few unguarded moments. This book seeks to draw attention to the value of safeguarding this often undervalued source of history.

Harry F. Byrd

CHAPTER 1

Why collect?

Few people need practical guidance on how to write a diary, even less on how to compose an interesting letter. Both the contents and the style of these documents will reflect the writer's own life and character; therein lies their charm and much of their value. This book is more concerned with persuading people of the advantages of preserving written and other memorabilia.

Items of intrinsic value are usually passed down from generation to generation. But what happens to everyday items which chronicle the daily life of past generations? When children grow up their childhood writing and records such as school books are usually discarded. At the time they may seem to be of little use – but what about fifty years on? Then such items may have considerable value as part of educational history as well as bringing the lives of parents or grandparents into focus for the following generations. What you record when you are young becomes history by the time you are old. A childhood diary, a sketchbook or a series of letters from an interesting moment or location, may become historically significant and even suitable for publication after ridiculously few years.

A page from Kathleen Strange's collection of illegible signatures.

When the older generation go there is no one left to answer the many questions that arise. After a bereavement there may be little time to sort out invaluable material from the mass of papers that must inevitably be destroyed. Few households have enough storage for everything of their own, much less from their parents' homes. This is how important records and vital letters are lost. The family history over a century or more can disappear in a few unguarded moments.

There are many reasons, however, why people today may not have the opportunity to collect. The distressingly common event of a broken home does not lend itself to the keeping of memorabilia. As parents are themselves divorced from each other, their children are divorced from their roots, Whole families lose their past in an age where mobility is a way of life, and they are deprived and impoverished because of it.

There is a store of suitable material lying around many homes waiting for that elusive time when there is enough time to 'do something about it'. "The first thing I would rescue in case of a fire (all things being equal of course) is my horde of memorabilia. It is beyond price and irreplaceable', said one friend. Research into the consequences of the Darwin Hurricane of 1984, found that those who had lost the memorabilia of their past life felt the most deprived – they felt that their roots had disappeared, and this affected them more profoundly than the loss of other, seemingly more valuable possessions. This was reported by Bill Bunbury in a lecture in Perth in 1994.

The title of this chapter comes from a piece written for this book by Kathleen Strange – a member of the Ephemera Society, and an arch collector if there ever was one. She wrote:

The question Why collect? has no simple answer. To put it another way – non-collectors see no point in embarking on a collection; they want to get rid of everything that is not a necessity. They dislike clutter, they tend to be over-tidy. It may be that they have lived in cramped surroundings and have not acquired the natural desire for space: there is no room in their homes for collectables. Collectors want to collect 'because it is there' though maybe this is not a valid reason.

To find others interested in one's own eccentricities brings a warm feeling of satisfaction. Perhaps one should not indulge oneself too much but try to discipline oneself not to overdo the collecting habit. If this thought should occur to you as you tidy up your shelves and cupboard, please bear in mind what an eloquent lecturer in social history said at a writers' conference: 'Never throw away your own records. If they must be disposed of ask a close relative or good friend to take responsibility. He or she may find some value in what you have been hoarding.' Finally, back to the question of why collect – I am reminded myself of the pleasures and surprises and mixed emotions I have had in sorting and sifting in collections of ephemera late in life.

One of my early collections concerned flying bombs. I collected everything about the 'doodlebugs' as they rained down on Kent in my early teens. I collected pictures and articles as well as pieces of wreckage from incidents. My prize exhibit was an undamaged gyroscope. Sadly my boxes did not survive. Over the years, my parents must have disposed of what appeared to be junk!

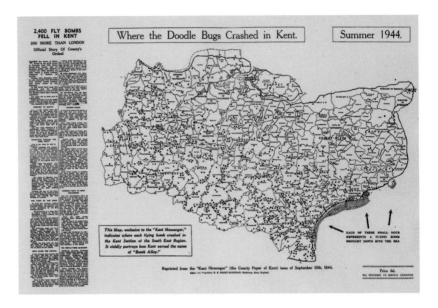

Kathleen, who died shortly before her hundredth birthday, had a wide range of collections. Items from several them are to be found in this book. Like her, we too may come to realise that what we thought was just an amusing hobby for ourselves may be of real value to scholars somewhere some day.

Other people would put different interpretations on why they might collect, or indeed what they might collect, and to what use they might expect their collection to be put to. Ruth Sebag Montefiore writes:

It is the tin boxes of family papers – the old letters and diaries, school reports, press cuttings, a memoir or two begun and then abandoned, that gets the adrenalin going – and it is never too late. All these papers formed the background to first book that I wrote when I was seventy, and led me on, like an animated sleuth, to more research in national libraries further afield. So the moral of this tale is never, never to throw anything away that might, one day, be of use to our descendants. Old school reports, if taken with a pinch of salt, are at least food for thought. Letters and diaries bring the subjects of those faded sepia photographs to life and the photographs themselves show how the family features, albeit altered here and there by new ingredients, repeat themselves over the generations; the whole collection providing an indispensable, rich harvest of material for students of the past.

I read with some amusement an article about collecting and collectors in the *Independent* a while ago. An Edinburgh professor, David Weeks, tried to define the type of people who collect: 'They have a higher IQ, an initially rigid moral

AIR FRANCE: LIORÉ-ET-OLIVIER H. 24-2 (France), a four-engined flying-boat used by Air France on its trans-Mediterranean services from Marseilles to Algiers and Tunis. It has a metal hull and wooden wings, with the four 350 h.p. Gnôme-Rhône K.7d engines mounted in two tandem pairs ... ings, where the

PLAYER'S CIGARETTES

AIR FRANCE : LIORE-ET-OLIVIER H. 24-2

WILLS'S CIGARETTES

GRACIE FIELDS

AIR FRANCE: POTEZ 62 (France). This is a twin-engined, twelve-passenger

GRACIE FIELDS. One of the most popular comediennes, the inimitable Gracie is Lancashire-born, and proud of it! She began her career by winning a singing competition at a local cinema when thirteen years old, and afterwards worked in a factory until she obtained a part in a touring revue with Archie Pitt. She and Archie soon left this, and their own show called "Mr. Tower of London," ran for seven years and played for more than 4,000 performances without a break. During this run she married Archie Pitt and has appeared in all his shows since. Gracie Fields first broadcast in 1927. (No. 31.)

code, and active fantasy life, difficulty dealing with irony and satire and barbed humour. They are scrupulous, perfectionist, conscientious and inclined to be obsessional.' 'Nonsense', replied Professor Susan Pearce, Professor of Museum Studies at the University of Leicester, 'It's not a suitable study for formal psychological analysis.' She added that thirty percent of the population are willing to describe themselves as collectors.

I would be inclined to go even further and ask you to consider whether collecting is not embedded deep in our genes – for some of us anyhow. It hurts us to dispose of anything that might be of use in the future, and the compulsion to collect is irresistible. What may have started in childhood as collecting cigarette cards, stamps, or pressed flowers and youthful diaries, progresses to something more important with age.

As well as collectors who amass memorabilia of historical or family interest, whether or not they may have any intrinsic value, there are those prudent people who keep their professional records or sketchbooks. These also can be invaluable to researchers in the future. Whatever the material, people who have a house full of family material may just happen to be the last in a line of relatives who have kept, rather than thrown away, such material. It is they who have the responsibility of deciding what to do with it all. They may get a lot of fun out of browsing through the material, and get real satisfaction about being in touch with their past. But they

Cigarette cards from the 1930s can reveal unexpected images and useful information, such as this picture of the young Gracie Fields. In amongst a random collection was An Album of International Air Liners which included an Air France flying boat.

Theatre programmes are indications of the collector's tastes and interests and can be of historical interest to those in that field of study.

have to decide if there are any of the next generation who would carry on the task, of caring for these archives – and if more than one, which one? If there is no one interested then it may be a matter of finding a museum, record office or other interested archive to entrust them to. They may have to consider the issues of conservation if precious documents are to be preserved in safety. If left to institutions there are other factors such as access and copyright to think about.

In quite a different field, helping the elderly to piece together memories, from written fragments and memorabilia from their past, reawakens a real sense of self esteem. This approach helps them to understand that their history is in itself a fragment of what social history is made of.

Chronicles are not only printed, written or drawn, but surely must include annotated photographic and transcribed oral records. I hope that this book will encourage people to keep as much as they can in the way of chronicles for their own sakes as well as for posterity. Too many people come to regret that they have 'spring cleaned' away so much of their past.

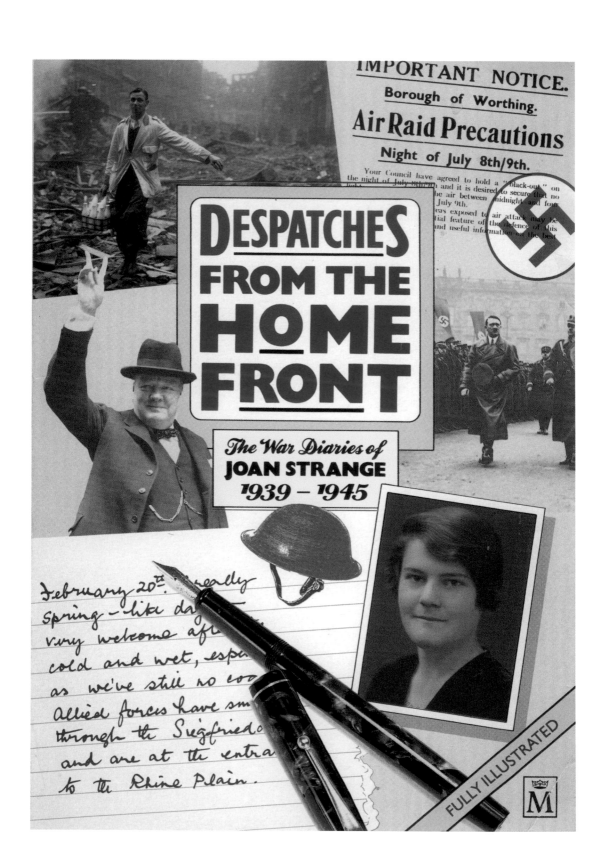

CHAPTER 2

Diaries

The importance of diaries, from Pepys to Anne Frank, among others, needs no introduction and no words of mine to underline their historical and social value. What we need to do today is to encourage people to keep records of their daily life. In our rushed existence and with the increasing use of computers, such mundane activities as diary keeping may well be laid aside and eventually be forgotten and disappear.

Do not underestimate the interest that there might be in your own diaries. During both the First and Second World Wars Kathleen Strange and her sister Joan both kept diaries. It all started this way as Kathleen described: 'In 1914, our form mistress had to give us something to do for the first ten minutes every day after prayers and before lessons proper started. "I want you to keep a war diary" she said. Rumours were already circulating that the war would be over by Christmas so we settled down to a term's work on war diaries. the eldest in the form could not have been more than twelve.' She continued: 'First as a schoolgirl, subsequently near middle

A page from Joan Strange's Second World War diary

A page from Joan Strange's First
World War diary. She was about
12 years old at the time.

Below: some examples from her
Second World War diary. They
add atmosphere to the text of
the diary

age, we collected newspaper cuttings, cartoons
and leaflets of advice about food rationing and
petrol and clothes restrictions. These numerous
papers illustrated the war diaries which were
written painstakingly throughout those years.
The diaries' entries included newspaper reports –

26

3,000,000 men. Germans driven back on the Yremen.
A burning trench at Malancourt. Germans hidden by smoke
Germany refuses officers to Turkey. Turkish troops hurried to Constantinople.
Mar 7th British ship sunk. Another fort in the Dardanelles silenced
Mar 8th Ex-sultan of Turkey escapes.
Mar 9th Pirates have sunk 3 British ships. 37 men missing.

German Zeppelin

900 ft.

British army dirigible

German military

including propaganda – and the effects of the wars on the civil population. From time to time, Joan Strange (the elder of the two sisters) had intended to throw the diary of the Second World War into the dustbin – but now her twelve volumes have been abridged and published with many illustrations, under the title *Dispatches from the Home Front*. Kathleen explained: 'Publication of her book bewildered my sister (by that time into her late eighties) who had no idea that her writings could have any value. The number of congratulations from known and unknown people have convinced her that she is responsible for a useful document of social history.' Sadly, Joan died soon after her diaries were published, but they are now in the possession of the Imperial War Museum.

French   English   Belgian
Serbian   Russian   Japanese

The Great European War Started on August 6th 1914

Kathleen Strange's First World War diary. She was about 10 years old at the time.

From Kathleen Strange's First World War diary, and below, from her sister's Second World War diary.

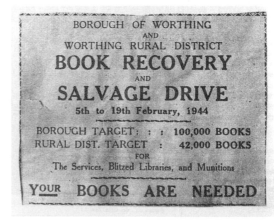

Harold Nicolson wrote an article about her sister, Joan and her war diaries in the *Listener* in 1937. It has been carefully preserved like everything else by these remarkable sisters. I would not agree with all he said, but it is an interesting comment: 'The seven little notebooks that I have in front of me would not merit publication, even in a parish magazine. They do not, as do the works of Mr Winston Churchill, provide one with a telescope through which one can survey the whole field of war from some sublime eminence …. These books in front of me provide rather a tiny pocket mirror — a two shilling piece of a looking glass — across which pass and repass the gigantic shadows of history …. And in her litltle notebooks one can follow the hopes and expectations, the dreads and disappointments, the lies and hatreds of that unhappy time.'

Both Harold Nicolson and his son Nigel, in a broadcast talk about diaries in 1969, stressed that: 'To begin with she believed everything, including the spy stories, which she was told by the popular press.' Kathleen Strange was far too modest to say much about her own diary of the First World War. It is a delightful document, full of childish illustrations.

A document, even if it reflects the effects of propaganda on a young newspaper reader, might be valuable — moreover diaries need not only be considered as material to be read by adults alone. A child's diary would be a wonderful resource for schools today. It was the 50th anniversary of the Second World War that

prompted the publication of Joan Strange's adult diaries. Perhaps we will have to wait for the centenary of the First World War in 2014, for someone to value these two unique childish documents enough to publish them.

Reading another war diary, *A Family Life 1939–45*, by Katherine Moore, published by Allison and Busby, one entry, for June 30th 1944, was of special interest. She had been describing the V1s, or doodlebugs, that were raining down on Kent at that time: 'Raids have been going on pretty continuously. It is very tiring at school and difficult teaching underground in stuffy dark trenches crouched on the wire bunks. A good many of the children have been sent away to safer districts. The poor School Certificate and Higher Certificate candidates had to do their exam papers either in the trenches or, if in the classrooms, to get down under their desks each time a bomb came over – sometimes five times in one paper! I was invigilating for an art exam when the form had to disappear several times beneath the desks and I saw one arm after another stretch out and up, grab their paper and paint brush and continue on the ground.' This brought back memories, as I was one of those doing my end-of-year exams in that school, in those trenches.

Sketches from F R Waley's diary written about 1913 during his time at Cambridge.

Katherine Moore was a prodigious writer. She wrote an account of her Edwardian childhood entitled *Queen Victoria is Very Ill* and co-authored, with the actress Joyce Grenfell, *An Invisible Friendship*. This book records the twenty-two year correspondence between them, yet they never met, keeping their friendship entirely on paper.

Diaries from any age are a source of fascination to a family, irrespective of whether they are suitable for publication or not. Where they are illustrated they provide even more interest. An example of this is the illustrated diary of my father, Frank Waley, documenting and illustrating the life and fashions in Cambridge (as seen through the eyes of a not very diligent student) in the years leading up to the First World War. It is now in the library of King's College Cambridge, where it is not easily accessible to his family, somewhat to their regret.

We never even saw my father's illustrated war diary. He donated it to his regimental museum. When the regiment was disbanded the diary disappeared completely. Be aware that, regrettably, this kind of thing can happen.

All such documents should be carefully preserved. Executors should note that they should be kept in the family wherever possible and preserved for future generations. Where there is no one interested in them – or no known descendants – then regional, if not national, libraries or record offices, are usually happy to receive and preserve such material in their archives.

An unusual set of diaries came into my possession when I was passing some time in an antiquarian bookshop, being early for an appointment in Adelaide, South Australia. They are six years of the records of a farmer – years that quite by coincidence cover the period of the First World War. What use could they possibly be, you might ask. To anyone interested in the history of agriculture they give a detailed picture of every day's farming activity in a town called Millicent.

Dr. MAY—Cash Account.

3	Set harness			
10	90ft Gal iron	4	10	0.
10	90ft Timber 15/-	4	0	0.
10	15ft 3x4 30		14	6.
10	3 pkts nails.		6	0
16	2 Lamps		6	0.
10	90ft Gal iron	4	0	0
11	12 bolts	4	10	0
13	1 bay colt.		12	0.
17	nails.	5	0	0.
17	Saw blade & handle		10	0.
18	27ft Gal iron.		3	10.
19	Income Tax Compiler bo	1	7	0.
19	Griffiths Bros.		10	6.
19	Osborne	1	9	3
19	Australasian	3	5	9.
19.	Tantanoola Rates.	1	6	8
25	1 Shovel.	3	6	0.
			8	0.

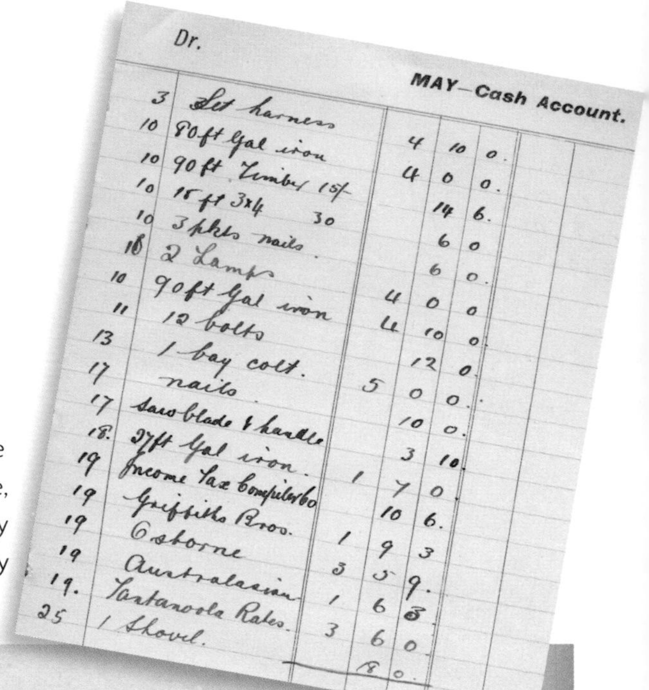

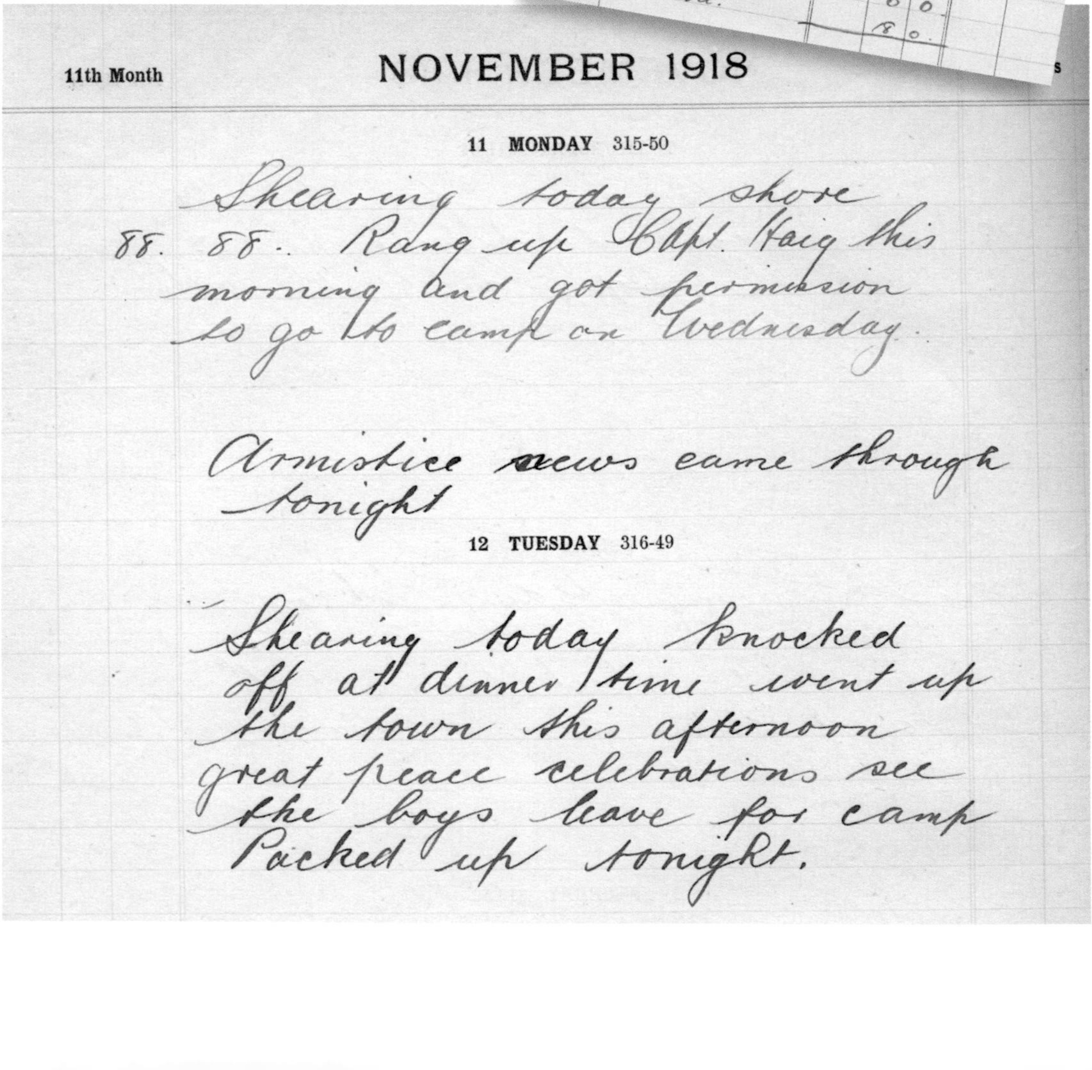

11th Month NOVEMBER 1918

11 MONDAY 315-50

Shearing today shore 88. 88.. Rang up Capt. Haig this morning and got permission to go to camp on Wednesday.

Armistice news came through tonight

12 TUESDAY 316-49

Shearing today knocked off at dinner time went up the town this afternoon great peace celebrations see the boys leave for camp Packed up tonight.

Diaries of a South Australian farmer. Notice the politically incorrect 'Why Trade with Foreigners'. The excerpt is written on Armistice day, 1918.

Inserts such as advertisements, sketches and children's notes add so much to these diaries and bring the times and characters into sharp focus.

Now let me go back to how I acquired them. I asked if the shop had any handwritten material, hoping for perhaps some schoolbooks. The man disappeared into a back room and came out saying something like: 'Are these any use? I am just about to dispose of them because they have been here for years and are taking up too much space.' It so happened that I was giving a talk at the state library that night and took these along. They caused an uproar — how dare I buy up their

Sowing, yields of wool or shearing, root crops, or hay are carefully noted — even on his wedding day. The covers alone would bring back names that older inhabitants might only half remember from their youth. Snippets of various kinds are clipped into the diary. A newspaper cutting of the funeral of the father of the diary writer, Chris Holland, would assist in tracing the family. This notice reveals that Mr D C Holland was born in England and arrived in the Millicent district in 1872. I have a good mind to try and trace the family myself. A serious researcher might compare the records and way of farming 80 years ago with the farming method on the same land today. I used an excerpt from the 1918 diary to illustrate Australian handwriting in a book entitled *Handwriting of the Twentieth Century*.

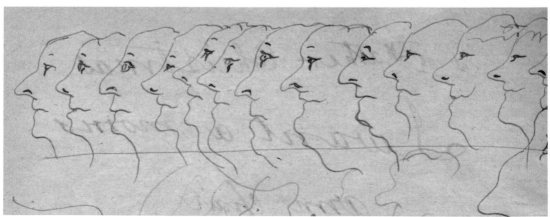

Who were the people portrayed here? Although names and addresses were found in the six volumes of these diaries, subsequent enquiries at the South Australian state library in Adelaide plus appeals in the local paper, failed to locate any descendents of the diarist.

> 'Dad wants a bigger morris arm chair nice & soft. so he can sleep in it.

> Dear Father Christmas I want a morris arm chair

heritage and take it away, etc. I tried to explain that they would soon have been destroyed forever because no one seemed to be interested, but the atmosphere was not very friendly. The diaries will eventually go back to the state library, (or the family if I can trace them) because that is where they belong. They document a fragment of Australia's history. Incidentally, some years later I returned to the shop and spied, in the window, the beautiful handwritten and illustrated maths book belonging to a long dead immigrant teacher – an equally important historical document in my view, once again ignored by those in the locality who might have valued it.

There are many other facets to diaries, and other uses that they can be put to. Genealogy is popular with professionals and amateurs alike but it is diaries and letters that bring characters from the past to life. It is not only the content of

A page from Eliza Keenan's diary of her life on a farm in Western Australia in the late 1870s

such records but the handwriting, even the implications suggested by the language, spelling or grammar, that interest many of us.

Keith McLeod used enlargements of pages of his great aunt's slightly earlier diary, from the other side of the country, around the walls of his bookshop in the Western Australian town of Margaret River. Today it is a popular tourist resort known for its surfing beaches and proximity to numerous vineyards. When the diary was written things were very different.

Keith McLeod writes: 'The author, Eliza

Unusually Eliza Keenan has added a contents to the end of her diary

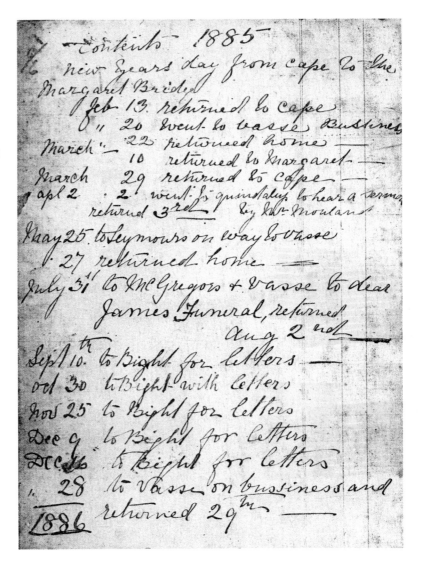

Keenan (known to her family as Lizzie) wrote these entries in 1885 as part of a diary she kept for over three years. Her family had come to the Margaret River area of Western Australia from Ireland in 1859. Lizzie was born in 1860, the second eldest of nine children. None of the kids went to school. (Margaret River was far too isolated in those days for such luxuries!) Lizzie, it seems, learned the rudiments of writing from her mother, Isabella.

During her childhood and teenage years Lizzie became increasingly responsible for helping to run and manage the family's farming concerns. Life was a harsh struggle at times, despite the fact that the Keenans' had brought some farming skills with them to the new country.

The diary entries on this page illustrate some of the day to day farming issues and, more poignantly, the stoic nature of Lizzie during the birth of her first child. The Mr A, referred to, is James Armstrong, her husband, who she had eloped with.

Fourteen years after these entries Lizzie died during the birth of her fourth child.'

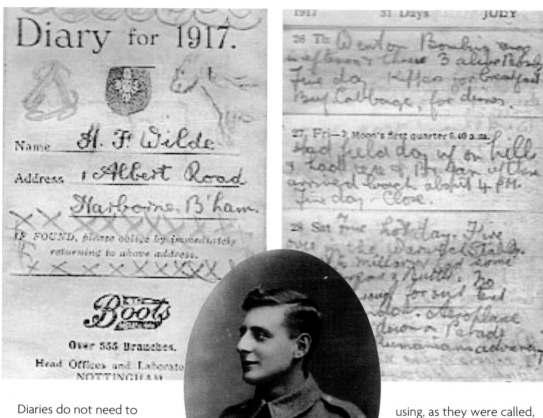

Diaries do not need to concern important personages to be important documents in their own right. They do not even have to record momentous periods in history to be interesting to future readers, although many that have survived seem to concern wartime in some way. Apart from being a wonderful source of reminiscence for the writer in later years, and a treasured possession for descendants in future generations, seemingly insignificant documents are important chronicles of social history and are becoming a rich source of material for research and publication.

Many diaries get discarded and turn up in strange places. Jean Weston found a small 1917 pocket diary in a box of bits and pieces bought in an auction sale. She describes it like this: 'All the entries have been written in pencil, often using, as they were called, one of the indelible kind which produced a smudgy purple-coloured ink when licked. It took many hours of patience and perseverance to transcribe this little book but, with the aid of a magnifying glass, gradually its contents unfolded. The diary tells, in minute detail all the happenings, likes and dislike of a young man in one momentous year, chronicling everything from a couple of months daily life, to his conscription in March, to the last days of 1917 and his arrival in Salonika from where he wrote: "Fifteen men broke out of camp and sentries were ordered to bayonet or shoot any trying to break out in the future."' 'These brief extracts from this fascinating book ignited my curiosity to learn more about H F. Had he survived the war and could he perhaps still be alive? Most

The 1917 diary that Jean Weston found in a box of bits and pieces led her to research the writer and locate his family.

> If you decide to lodge your family diary in a suitable archive, make sure that everyone knows where it is so that future generations are able to access it.

importantly, however, was the need to know the actual name of the young man who had kept his own unique chronicle of the year he became a soldier of the Great War.' Jean is an inveterate researcher. She not only traced his family and amassed photographs and a complete record of his later life, she is now preparing all this for publication.

The discovery of one such diary was reported in several national newspapers in the spring of 1995. It was written by a servant – a £10 a year housemaid – between the years 1911 and 1922 when she died of tuberculosis at the age of 30, her health broken by the tragedy of the break up of her engagement in the turmoil of the First World War. The diary is augmented with the postcards sent from the front. The diary was to be used (as reported in *The Times* of March 8 1995) as a centrepiece of an exhibition in Dorchester Record Office to mark the centenary of the National Trust. 'It is a remarkable piece of work which throws light on life below the stairs', said a spokeswoman. Beatrice's papers will be published in book form by the National Trust, stated the *Daily Mail* in an article entitled 'How a Jilted Servant Girl Died of a Broken Heart'.

A diary chronicling every day life in 1948 turned up in a Brixton skip some years ago. It was written by a Fulham publican's wife struggling to inject a little drama and romance into the drab austerity of post-war London. It became the subject of an exhibition entitled: 'Diary of an Unknown Woman'. It was described this way: 'This exhibition was inspired by her thoughts, obsessions and the day-to-day rituals of her married life.' There was talk of turning it into a film. This shows that, even if you or your descendants jettison your diary, it may end up being used unexpectedly in some way, somewhere and some time.

An extension of the idea of what to do with a diary, found not in a skip this time but at a car boot sale, was illustrated in a newspaper article in 1988. The finder was intrigued at the diary of a young boy, written in 1944, labelled 'Private Do Not Open'. He paid £1 and did open it. Apart from the interest of the contents which showed that the young boy had followed the progress of the war keenly, the article deals with the extraordinary story of how the finder traced the writer, now aged 65. They finally met – one to be delighted to have his boyhood memories returned, and the other to enjoy the satisfaction of a happy ending to his search. What about the humble office diary? The diary keeper for an important personage wields a lot of power. Some people might think such documents are better destroyed at the end of each year – but others not so. It is not long ago that a prominent politician was convicted with the help of evidence recorded in his office diary. Some businessmen's diaries are confined to dates and prices. That may be all they need to remind themselves of happenings, but without words they would be useless to others, but perhaps secrecy is the real reason for their brevity.

When you start to keep a diary you never know where it will lead you but if you never start you will never find out. Where and how it ends up, however, may not be entirely your decision.

Dear J.G. (yes - I like the use of initials - I was always called by mine at school.)

Thank you so much for your second handkerchief letter. Handkerchiefs are a sore point with me just now as I am in bed with one of the most furious colds ever invented. That is why I am afraid this may be rather a long letter. Now - this morning, to cheer me up, comes another letter with your poems. I like

JOYCE GRENFELL
KATHARINE MOORE
An Invisible Friendship
an exchange of letters 1957-1979

CHAPTER 3

Letters

Letters are the mainstay of biographers and historians – but will this repertoire of vital and detailed information be available for posterity? The telephone began to replace many personal letters, polite notes or love missives. Our grandparents habit of exchanging frequent, maybe daily, written messages between family and friends began to fade. Now the fax, e mail and text messages have taken over. These are convenient for the sender and result in ever more flippant exchanges of personal information – but to call them even ephemeral is to over-emphasise their lasting quality.

In the event of having to clear out a deceased relative's house, old letters are likely to be one of the first casualties. I am not suggesting that either the attic or desk will necessarily yield much of intrinsic value, but to that young relative who is beginning to thirst for knowledge about his or her ancestors, or the local museum, they might be very valuable. Even if you are not going to be able to store them indefinitely I urge you to take a good look at each one before you jettison everything. You may end up getting involved in something of great personal interest in spite of yourself.

Many people assiduously research their family tree. They may get obsessed with tracing every last connection, every date and place of birth, marriage or death. At the same time they often ignore the letters that would fill in the intriguing details of their ancestor's lives. Handwritten correspondence provides another dimension. You do not need to be a graphologist to experience that thrill when you recognise the writing of a friend on a long expected envelope. That same feeling is more poignant when you see something written by a much loved relative, long dead. Their handwriting brings them back in a singular way. It is a reflection of themselves on paper, and no two scripts are exactly the same. So through the written trace of your ancestors, although you never knew them, can be glimpsed

The cover of *Invisible Friendship*, a book that records the twenty-two year correspondence between these two remarkable women who never met.

The Young Ambassadors was compiled from the letters of a young girl evacuated to America during the Second World War

their characters. They begin to feel familiar, to be real people not just names on a family tree.

Once again, I am not so concerned with the correspondence of famous people. This book concentrates on what might be found in almost anyone's cupboard. It gives an idea of what can be done with this information and what satisfaction can result through either reading it for your own interest, developing it for some purpose or finding an appropriate resting place for it.

One of my early teenage memories is of buying a book called *The Young Ambassadors*. Its price, 12/6, would have made a considerable hole in my finances in 1944 when I was aged 13. Its

significance to me was that the writer was about my own age and we had had very similar experiences. We had both been evacuated to America during the war. The difference between us was that her parents had kept all the letters that she had written home during those years apart, and my parents had not. Angela Pelham's book was based on those letters. I still have this modest wartime economy standard book, all yellow brown with age, and wonder if she later became a professional writer. Those childhood letters were well written and have stood the test of time.

In 1990, to mark the half a century since we all were evacuated, the Imperial War Museum published a volume of letters by other transatlantic evacuees entitled *Special Relations*. Some of these letters were reproduced so their gradual change-over to the American style of handwriting is documented, which particularly interested me. Somehow the museum got hold of my name and I was invited to the launch. This led to a request from my local radio station for a talk to add to their oral archive. Sadly, my talk relied only on my memory of events fifty years ago, and none of the vivid details that would have been recorded in letters.

I must have complained loudly to my long suffering parents, who would have had many other concerns during the war years. Anyhow, they never forgot and when the occasion arose for another prolonged absence they kept all the letters that I wrote home. This was when I was first married and went to live in Uganda for several years. Reading them now provides

This and next few pages show a small part of an archive of letters and allied information written by a Portuguese diplomat from the siege of Paris in 1870 and 1871.

immediate recall of events – and there were quite significant ones in those years leading up to independence – that would otherwise have been forgotten. However, having spent a self-indulgent day ploughing through them, I feel that they are more interesting just to me and my immediate family than posterity.

Some letters appear insignificant but contain vital information, while others may look beautiful and that is all. This collection of letters to my great-grandfather, were written by Navarro d'Andrado, a Portuguese diplomat, during the siege of Paris in 1870 and 1871. This collection is perhaps more important for the provenance than for the letters themselves. It also is a good example of how to collect and organise a small archive. Each letter or other document has been

Navarro Andrado and his signature. Below is a rough translation from one letter that reads: 'In spite of small personal problems, at least I have not yet eaten Coco, or burned my furniture. All this will be nothing if France is saved.'
'Bien des petites miseres personelles – bien que je n'ai pas encore devoré Coco ni brulé mes meubles … Tout cela ne sera rien si la France se sauve.'

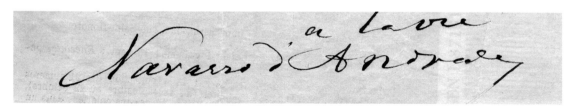

All this is part of an interesting
archive carefully collated and
annotated by my grandfather.
It includes this Lettre-Journal
whose content would, no doubt,
be of interest to historians.

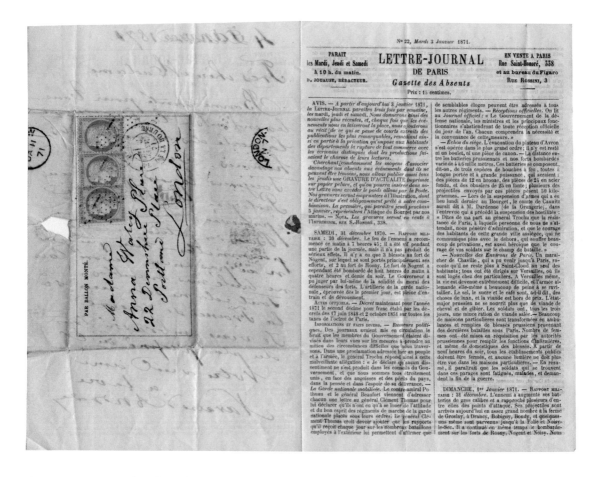

kept in a separate, dated envelope, annotated
with additional notes by three generations of the
family who can be identified by their handwriting.
Admittedly it would take an expert to decipher
and translate all of the spidery and faded writings.
The facts need to be extracted from the
excessively flowery language, but after that a
detailed picture of the daily trials and tribulations
would emerge. The sentence on the previous
page, came from a letter from Navarro Andrado
to my great grandmother. It was written on the

back of a Lettre-Journal obviously printed for the
purpose.

The provenance of one of the letters alone is
worth recording. There is a printed notice, dated
3rd December 1870, from F C Jackson JP, of St
Ruan Rectory. Helston, Cornwall. It states: 'The
enclosed, among many others [letters], was
washed ashore at the Lizard, supposed to come
from the Balloon reported off the Eddystone'....
Then on the back of the envelope it says: 'Picked
up at sea off the Lizard by a poor fisherman. Any

These illustrations tell of a remarkable sequence of events. The mail from Paris was transported by balloon one of which came down off the coast of Cornwall. Some of its contents were rescued by a fisherman. He reported his find to a local dignitary who forwarded this envelope to my great grandfather with a request for a reward for the fisherman.

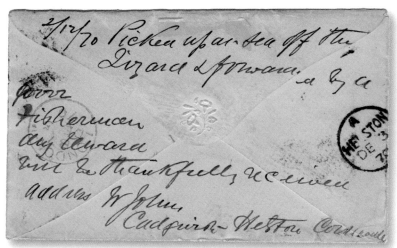

ST. RUAN RECTORY,
HELSTON, CORNWALL,
December 3rd, 1870.

The enclosed, among many others, was washed ashore at the Lizard, supposed to have come from the Balloon reported off the Eddystone. I have taken the liberty of forwarding it in a clean Envelope, as many of the Letters are greatly injured by the Sea.

I shall be obliged by your forwarding me the Stamp thus expended, and anything you may feel inclined to give to the Fishermen who took them from the waves.

Yours Faithfully,
F. C. JACKSON, J.P.

POST OFFICE TELE

Regulation as to Inland Telegrams.

If the Receiver of an Inland Message doubts its accuracy, he may have it
of its transmission to him. In the event of an error having been made, the an
refunded on application to the Secretary.

Office of Origin _Boulogne_ 4   Handed in at _7.36._

From _B. Gosselin_   To _S._

Words	Charge	
20	1/-	_The line from Boulogne_
		the transmission of all g
		revictualling of Paris it i
		smoked and salted mea
25	1/3	_in a small volume will_
30	1/6	_preference. The President_
35	1/9	_of Boulogne can deliver th_
40	2/-	_for sending the said goods by b_

When the cost of a reply to a Telegram has been prepaid, and the number of words in the reply is in ex
words over the number so prepaid. The reply must be handed in at the Office from which the original Telegr
  A prepaid reply to a Message must be handed in within two days from the date of the original Message,
returned on application to the Secretary.
  Telegrams may be re-directed from town to town at an extra charge of _one-half_ the ordinary inland tari
they must not have been opened.
    N.B.—It will materially assist the Department if, in making any inquiry respecting this Telegram
of a Foreign Message, the application should be addressed to the Administration to

Jas. Truscott & Son, London.

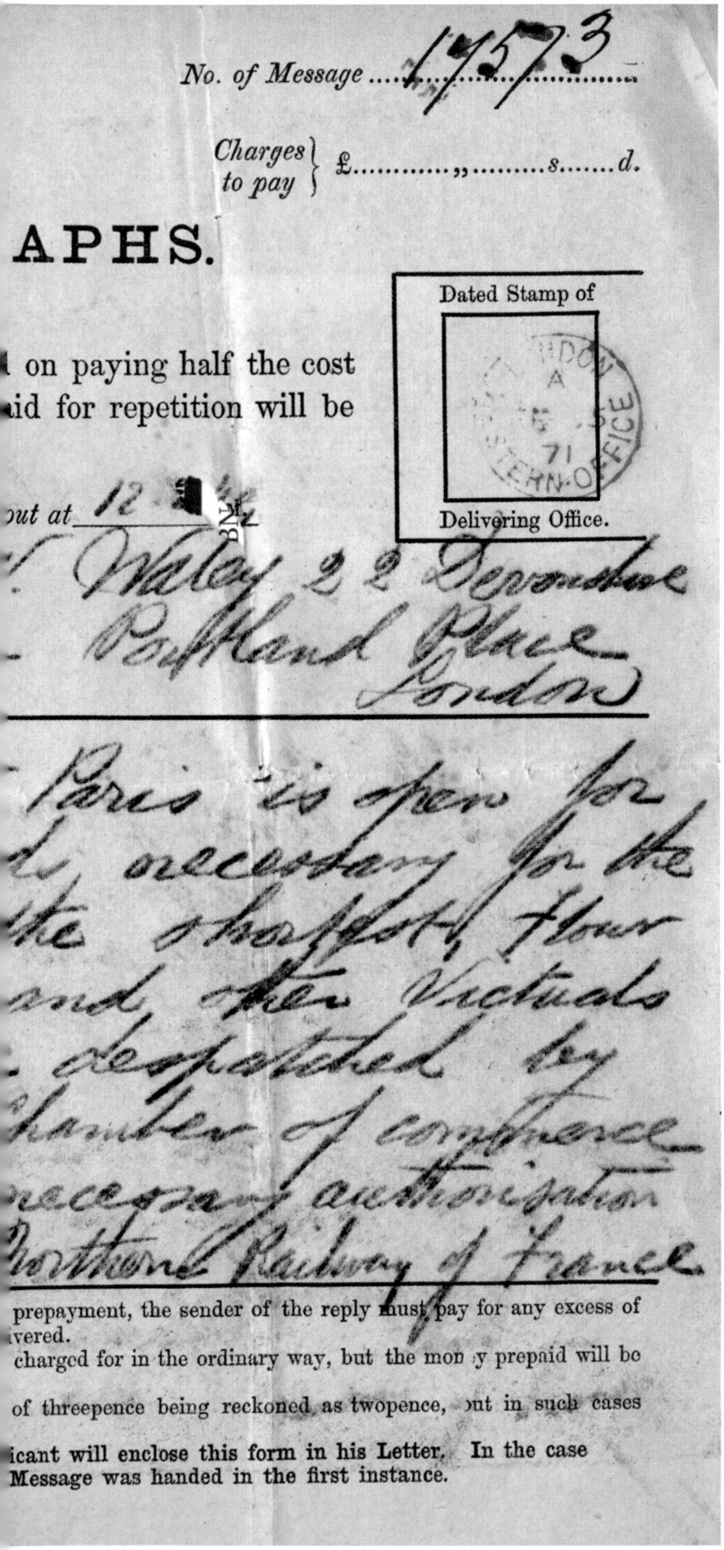

No. of Message *1573*

Charges } £..........,,........s......d.
to pay }

APHS.

on paying half the cost
id for repetition will be

Dated Stamp of

Delivering Office.

ut at *12*

Waley 2 2 Devonshire
Portland Place
London

Paris is open for
necessary for the
shortest, Flour
other Victuals
despatched by
chamber of commerce
necessary authorisation
Northern Railway of France

prepayment, the sender of the reply must pay for any excess of
vered.
charged for in the ordinary way, but the money prepaid will be
of threepence being reckoned as twopence, but in such cases
icant will enclose this form in his Letter. In the case
Message was handed in the first instance.

Another illustration from this archive which is a good example of how such memorabilia should be preserved. Telegrams also have a part to play in archives. All too often they brought bad tidings in times of war, but this carefully preserved one (though the exact date in 1871 has been obscured) provides details about food shortages in Paris. The form also records the regulations and charges for telegrams at that time.

I have to question the judgement of the expert who announced that all these documents were of little value because so many are still around. A researcher of that period might not agree either.

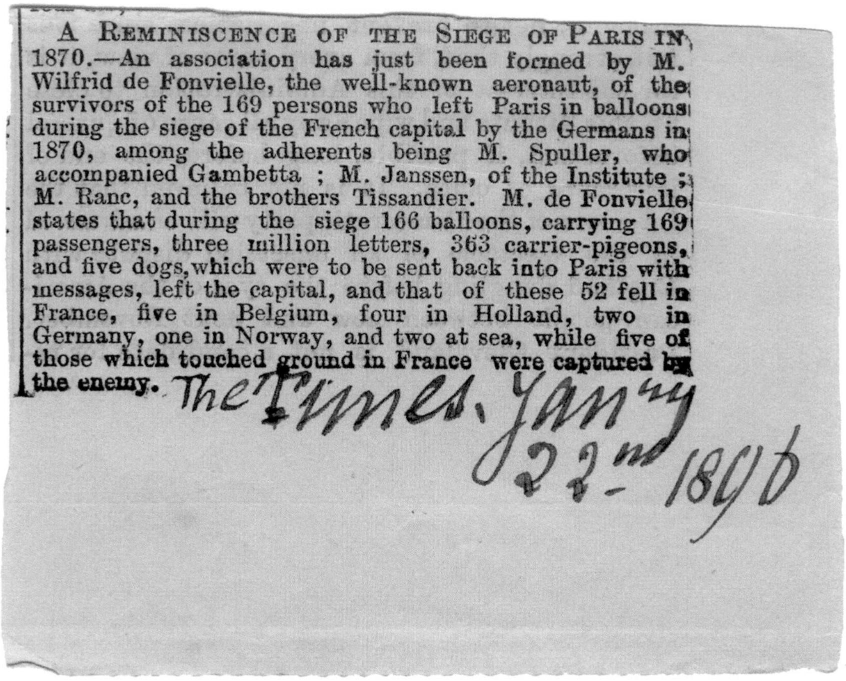

A REMINISCENCE OF THE SIEGE OF PARIS IN 1870.—An association has just been formed by M. Wilfrid de Fonvielle, the well-known aeronaut, of the survivors of the 169 persons who left Paris in balloons during the siege of the French capital by the Germans in 1870, among the adherents being M. Spuller, who accompanied Gambetta ; M. Janssen, of the Institute ; M. Ranc, and the brothers Tissandier. M. de Fonvielle states that during the siege 166 balloons, carrying 169 passengers, three million letters, 363 carrier-pigeons, and five dogs, which were to be sent back into Paris with messages, left the capital, and that of these 52 fell in France, five in Belgium, four in Holland, two in Germany, one in Norway, and two at sea, while five of those which touched ground in France were captured by the enemy.

The Times, Jan'ry 22nd – 1896

A report of the balloon post from *The Times*. And a note in my grandfather's handwriting enclosed in this archive, describing its content.

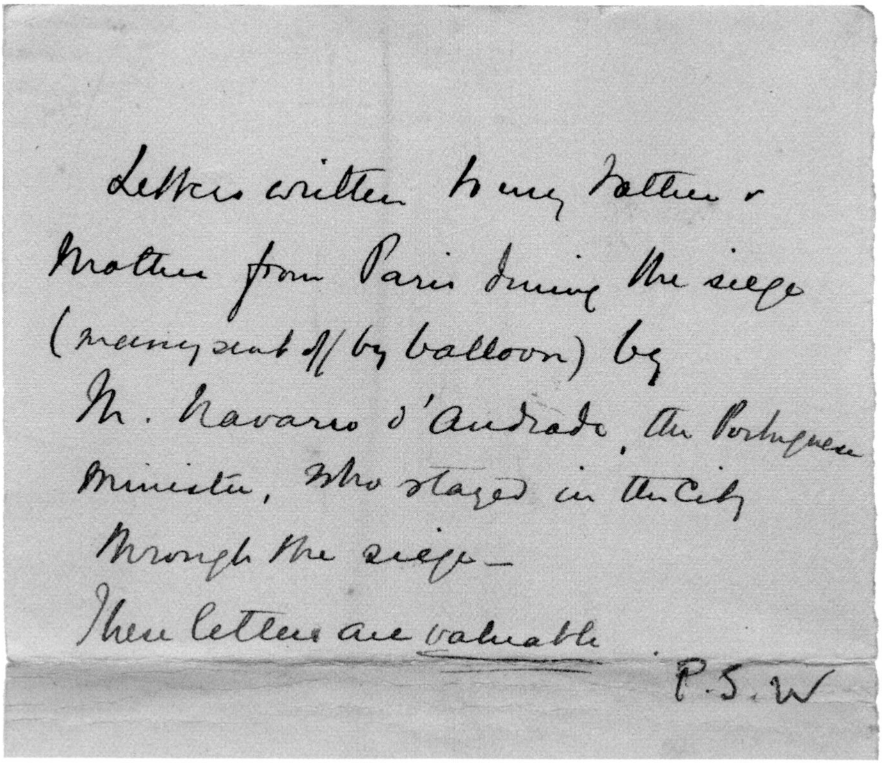

Letters written to my Father & Mother from Paris during the siege (many sent off by balloon) by M. Navarro d'Andrade, the Portuguese Minister, who stayed in the City through the siege—

These letters are *valuable*

P.S.W

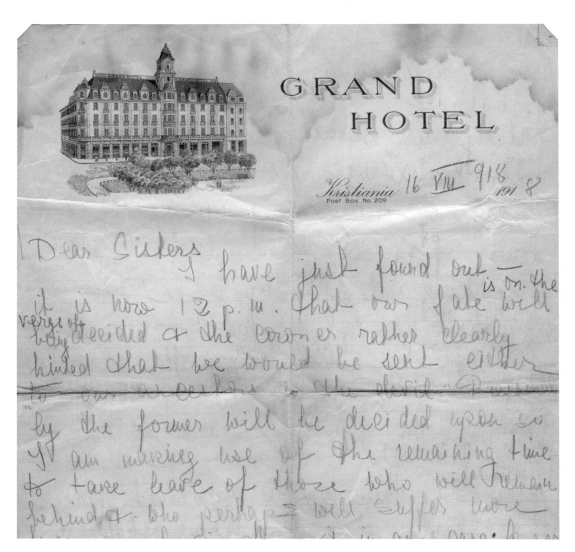

GRAND
HOTEL

Kristiania 16 VIII 918 1918
Post Box No. 209

Dear Sisters I have just found out —
it is now 12 p.m. that our fate will is on the
verge of being decided & the coroner rather clearly
hinted that we would be sent either
to our ancestors or the devil ...
"by the former will be decided upon so
I am making use of the remaining time
to take leave of those who will remain
behind & who perhaps will suffer more

Part of a contemporary translation of a letter from a relative about to be executed during the Russian Revolution in 1918. This is something treasured by the family as a remembrance of a very brave man.

reward will be thankfully received'. There are also newspaper cuttings that report the incident.

Another newspaper cutting, dated 22nd January 1896 (in my grandfather's hand) adds another dimension to the story. It reports the formation of an asssociation of the survivors of the 169 persons who left Paris during the siege in balloons. It tells of 166 balloons which carried three million letters and three hundred and sixty carrier pigeons and, inexplicably, five dogs.

We must be thankful to the three generations who saved and annotated this collection, all carefully stored in separate envelopes.

The first letter written by Marion Richardson to Benenden School in 1923, from a collection of correspondence in the school's archive.

We have another letter from the other side of the family that chronicled another time of war and suffering. A brave young man, about to be executed by the Bolsheviks during the revolution in Russia, wrote a last letter home. The original, written in Russian has long since been lost but his nieces translated the original letter for the sake of their English-speaking relatives. I have my late godmother's faded copy. At the time it was written, she and her family had just escaped overland from St Petersburg into Scandinavia. Somehow the faded letter heading and Lucie's teenage handwriting and hesitant translation, seem to make this even more vivid.

> Old letters are by nature usually rather frail. If many members of the family want to inspect them it might be a good idea to make copies to preserve the originals.

Recently, I have had experience of the use of correspondence to help in writing a biography. I was asked to write a life of the pioneer educationist Marion Richardson. There were plenty of articles concerning her actual work on child art and handwriting, but next to nothing on her personal life or character. It was a matter of delving into archives to find any surviving letters.

The main archive was in Birmingham and the letters that interested me the most were between her and the famous calligrapher Edward Johnston. They had never been published or even apparently been properly catalogued or looked at (except by a student many years ago). The only interest appeared to be in the child art side of her

work. These letters revealed how she had constantly asked for his advice during the preparation for her Dudley Writing Cards. They reveal his patience and kindness correcting her samples while at the same time, he seemed to be warning her not to stick too close to his work which, after all was aimed at the professional scribe or letterer, not children. He wrote:

> I think that is what has been happening in regard to my advice. My principles are real – I am convinced – I can do & apply them to my own work, but the subtle differences in their application to a seemingly similar, but really different, kind of work, are probably very difficult to apprehend. In such differences principles must appear to suffer modification…. In short, it seems to me that my recent advice to you has been misleading & that you could do better without it: that you have some conscious or instinctive knowledge of what is required.

Marion Richardson ignored Johnston's advice and her cards copied his calligraphic style and were not very successful with children.

Letters can tell more than their actual contents. I had formed certain feelings about her complex character but needed confirmation. Graphologist, Elaine Quigley, reviewed a collection of Richardson's letters at various stages in her career and confirmed much of what I had suspected: that she was a perfectionist, lacking emotion and passion, controlling and disliking argument and contradiction – and many more useful insights.

5th Sept. '23

Dear Miss Sheldon,

After seeing you I wrote at once to Miss Fountain but have only now received her reply. Miss Fountain is unwilling to give advice as to salary but suggests £30 for the first term and I am willing to take her opinion in the matter and accept £30 plus travelling expenses. This is considerably less than Burnham Scale or the rate paid by the L.C.C. to visiting mistresses but then your numbers will at first be small.

Another remarkable collection of letters came from the archives of Benenden School. They cover the entire eight years that she taught there. The first letter is of interest as it defines her expectation of salary etc. but it is the comparison between the first and the last example that is the most telling. You would not need to be a graphologist to discern the deterioration in her script which somehow fortells her actual decline into ill health a few years later (sometimes attributed to over work), leading to a final breakdown.

Many letters that have been treasured are from times of war. My father kept, all through his life, a poignant letter from his Uncle Fred. He must have been about six years old at the time that Fred set off for the Boer War, writing: 'I have a sort of idea that we shall not be back in England for a good many years.' He died at Spion Kop.

Elizabeth Talbot Rice, who worked for the National Army Museum, once said to me: 'The most infuriating thing is to hear that someone has left some interesting letters and then to be just too late and find that the relatives have disposed

Some of the nineteenth century letters kept by family members. It is quite an emotional experience to read these personal notes – but who will keep them in the future?

of them.' Today, however it is so easy to photocopy or scan any documents that someone in the family may wish to keep a little longer. Then a copy can be lodged in the appropriate archive in case of future loss.

That is one side of the question, but there is another. It is just not possible to keep everything. How can you decide which ordinary, personal letters to keep and which to get rid of? Things that are meaningful to one or two generations often lose their meaning after several more. There are times when my house feels like a giant dustbin. I come from generations of amassers. When my father died, I asked for anything handwritten to be kept, but did not expect the sackloads that appeared. Not only were there letters but address books, visitors books, autograph albums, beautiful deeds and marriage settlements, wills, bills, codicils and so much more. After I thought I had finished this chapter a

Letters from friends and relatives no longer with us immediately bring the writer back to mind.

Will emails and text messages ever have the same impact in the future?

large packet of letters surfaced in a sack of oddments. I opened it and found, amongst other things, a letter to my grandfather from his grandmother on his twenty-first birthday. It looks as fresh as if it were written yesterday. It is quite emotional to find something like that from the hand of my great great grandmother, my children's great great great and their six children's great great great great grandmother. But what will they want to keep of the personal correspondence of their distant ancestors and how will they manage to preserve them as carefully as past generations have? That is something that they will have to resolve like every other family faced with the same problem.

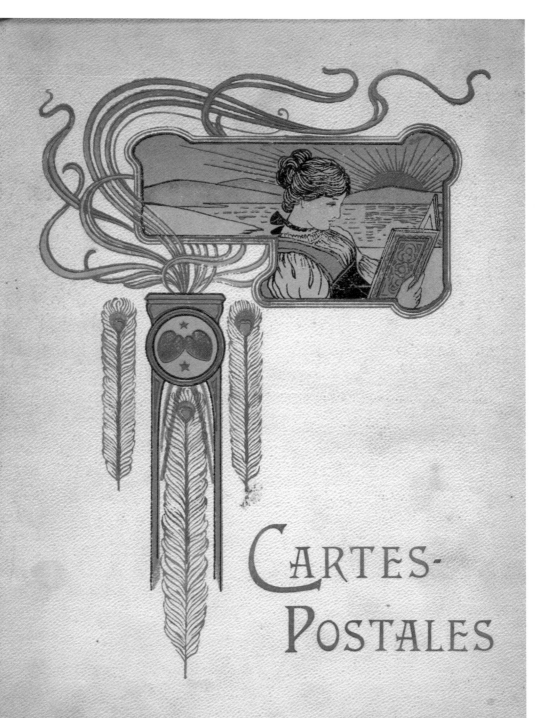

CARTES-
POSTALES

CHAPTER 4

Postcards and even envelopes

Collecting postcards was a fashionable occupation in late Victorian and Edwardian times in particular. An elderly lady showed me one such album many years ago. It consisted of interminable seaside views, of great interest to the collector no doubt, who appeared to have time to kill and plenty of money, judging from the impressive exterior of the album. The images were, however, of limited interest to others (as are a friend's holiday photographs today). But what about the reverse side of the postcards? They might reveal an interesting record of the holiday activities of leisured ladies of that period.

The cover of an early twentieth-century postcard album.

The written side of postcards reveals much more than that. They provide, for instance, evidence of the incredible efficiency of mail deliveries. One postcard shows how confident in the service someone's Aunt Emily of Loughborough Rd was when she wrote to Dear Ivy at 37 New Bond St, saying: 'Can you come round this afternoon and listen in the shop while I do things up stairs?' An article in *The Times* entitled 'Love letters by mail – 12 times a day?' tells us that in 1914, for instance, the Post Office offered up to twelve deliveries a day in central London with up to seven in the suburbs. Sadly this service declined during World War One to seven a day and never recovered. Other details about postal services came to light in my youngest aunt's memoirs: 'In one half of the front door was a flat letterbox, not openable from the inside, and from which two postal collections were made daily, at 2pm and midnight. This service cost two pounds per annum and you could choose which of the two collections of the day you wished to use. Deliveries in the day numbered five' (in 1920). Now we are lucky to get one delivery!

It was not only in London, or Great Britain for that matter, and not only in terms of speed that the legend on the back of postcards reveals how efficiently everything was expected to work within postal services. A card addressed only to James Halby Esq, solicitor, Cambridge (New

The back of this non-assuming picture postcard reveals the efficiency of the postal service in London at the time that it was posted.

The writer assumed that it would be delivered in time for the recipient to act on the message that same afternoon.

Zealand, not England) obviously expected the post office to locate him and do it quickly because on the other side is a message which says: 'Case of figs on to-days train'. Jessie, the writer obviously does not expect the fruit to have to sit at the station too long. Another card from this same collection (belonging to a friend who now lives in Australia) shows how a lazy commercial traveller did not even have to exert himself to write to a customer on one side – or put too much of an address on the other.

A judicious mix of the front and reverse of post cards within a collection can reveal so much family history. I have just been going through the collection made by my mother and uncle at the turn of the century. My Russian grandfather was

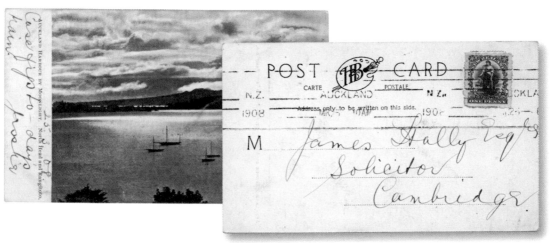

Above: The writer of this card also expected a fast postal delivery in New Zealand – otherwise the case of figs in the message on the left would not last long.

Two more cards from New Zealand.

A selection of postcards from a child's collection from various countries, like this one from St Petersburg, has made it possible to trace the travels of this family at an interesting time of their lives.

a diplomat and although we know the outline of his travels the postcards fill in some fascinating details. The first from St Petersburg was dated 1902 when he was recalled home but his family were still in London. Incidentally it was an appropriate card to send to a little boy – a picture of the Hermitage, perforated in certain places so that when it was held up to the light the scene was illuminated. Two years later they were ensconced in their Kentish home at Iden Manor, only, according to the postcards, to be posted to Washington by 1904. They were still there in 1905 as more postcards followed to and from the nearby Kent villages of Staplehurst and Frittenden, referring to their transatlantic trips. On the back of one is the message: 'I expect you are a real sailor by now.' I must take this collection of views (much more beautifully reproduced than modern ones) next time I visit that area and compare the views.

Another picture postcard shows that they are back at Iden in 1905. My grandmother must have become used to packing and unpacking because by 1906 they were at the Embassy in Tokyo. One postcard sent to them (and carefully kept by the children) says Japan via Brindisi, another Japan via San Francisco (whereas the family had travelled via the trans-Siberian railway). This was, of course, before air travel and neither post nor long distance travel could have been simple.

Two extraordinary cards from Tokio (as it seems to have been spelled then), have a message on the back in my grandfather's hand, noting: 'Stamps and postcards issued for ten days only during the last Emperor of Japan's coronation.' This might place these journeys in an exact historical perspective, but the date on the cards puzzled me – 4.11.19. By the time of the Russian Revolution my grandparents were back in Washington. A friend suggested that in Japan, at

CARTE POSTALE

Stamps & post cards issued for ten days only during the last Emperor of Japan's coronation

One card from Japan had some interesting stamps on it – but no one can tell me which emperor is referred to.

Below: Some of the older picture post cards are of interest to local archives. If necessary these can be scanned for them so as to preserve the post card collection.

that time, they might have used American date notation. 19.4.11 looks better but is still not right. Investigations continued after a friend who has spent many years in Japan related that where we would put the year – 19.. – Japanese would indicate the year in the reign of the emperor. Accordingly this date would then indicate 1877 in the reign of Meiji 0r 1923 in the reign of Taisho. So, maybe these were just part of a collection – but still, which emperor's coronation?

The postcards now become of interest to postal history as well as family or the Kent County Library (museums as well as record offices sometimes appreciate local views of a century ago). I discussed this collection with the rural studies librarian and was heartened by her reply. 'Bring them along and we will scan them in and add any we need to our collection.' So nowadays you do not even have to donate anything that a future member of the family might value.

Each of these postcards reveals an unusual snippet of information, and could lead anyone who had the interest and time to follow them, into further research.

This envelope (one of several) from a prisoner of war camp, came from my grandfather's stamp collection. They led to an interesting story and it was possible to restore one of them to the family of the writer for their own archive. Sadly, the letters that had once been inside the envelopes had not been kept.

Now on to envelopes and what you might find in stamp albums. This section carries the same message: 'Never throw away or sell anything without a good look first.' Stamp collectors frequently keep envelopes while most others discard them. Philatelists may value them mostly for the stamps – but what about the contents or other matters concerning family or history that they may reveal?

A trawl through a quite unexceptional stamp collection found a dozen or so envelopes tucked loosely in between the pages. Some Second World War envelopes with military censor stickers excited a friend who specialises in military philately, but several deserved closer inspection. They came from a British internment camp in Algeria, dated 1942. They were decorated with portraits of Marshal Petain plus impressive official red rubber stamps. Some were from the Centre D'Interment but others, for some reason, bore the stamp of the Regiment of Spahis, The letters

reached England by air from Marseilles – how, in the middle of the war, is a bit of a mystery. Perhaps they came via Lisbon but the censorship sticker hid that bit of information each time.

It was too late to reunite these envelopes with the sender, but it was not too hard to locate his family, to see if they wanted these small glimpses of their family history. They might even have kept the letters that came inside these envelopes. A fascinating story emerged of a naval officer on the Malta convoys, whose ship was torpedoed. While returning to England on another ship it ran aground in North Africa – hence a naval officer in a prisoner-of-war camp in Algeria.

A rather florid envelope, commemorating the first air mail service to Australia in 1931, revealed a beautifully written letter from our Great Uncle Fred. He had emigrated to Australia very early in the century because, as family gossip has it, his family disapproved of his bride. As it happened, Uncle Fred did very well indeed for himself in

Don't forget to look inside those attractive first day covers. They may be hiding interesting letters.

Below: Some more postal history, all on the reverse of a picture postcard dated 1934.

lovely envelope that is headed Tin Can-Canoe Island. (It is even possible to guess who, from the handwriting.) Apparently Niuafoou, or Tin Can Island, one of the Tongan group, did not have a proper harbour in those days (1934). Steamers, in this case the SS *Monterey*, had to throw the mail overboard in a tin container. My envelope indicates that this was a ship of the Oceanic Line, plying from Hawaii and the South Seas to New Zealand and Australia. These Australian memorabilia will be treasured by my two daughters and four grandchildren who are now Australian citizens.

Such fragments would be of little interest to those dealers who might relieve the elderly or their relatives of their collections to break up and dispose of as profitably as possible. However, many such snippets of information must be languishing in collections. They could bring detail and colour to family and social histories for those who know where to look.

Sydney. In a box of assorted bits more transpired about him.

Correspondence kept in the collection because of the unusual stamps, dated 1907, show that one of his brothers was on the way to visit him, stopping in at Tonga on the way. It must have been quite an adventure then. According to the messages on the back of two cards the traveller was not at all enthralled with Tonga, despite staying at the Residency. One says: 'We are here but as usual wet and hot.' The other, written several days later: 'We leave here today, our last stopping place, and I will not be sorry to leave.' (Perhaps those cards belonged in the last section – but they fit so well in here.)

The next generation evidently followed the same route to the Antipodes. This is revealed by a

TAMARA

*Memoirs of
St Petersburg,*

Paris,

Oxford

and

Byzantium

TAMARA TALBOT RICE

Edited by Elizabeth Talbot Rice

JOHN
MURRAY

CHAPTER 5

Memoirs

Famous people, politicians in particular, seem to spend their retirement writing their memoirs, but what about other people? This subject does not only concern the great and famous, and what actually constitutes a memoir? I suppose a memoir is almost anything from a full autobiography, a biography written by a second person to short jottings of any aspect of life recorded for grandchildren, or perhaps written to be published in a parish magazine. Apart from their importance to history, memoirs are what make a person interesting to their descendants, and come alive again perhaps many years or even centuries after their life has ended.

This chapter shows how different approaches to and levels of memoirs all have importance. Sometimes substantial notes and written memories are left for someone else to edit and include additional material, then what would that be – a biography, or a memoir – does it matter? The cover of one such publication is illustrated here. It is Elizabeth Talbot Rice's skilful editing of her mother's manuscript. 'Encouraged by family and friends my mother began writing her memoirs in the mid-1970s.... Had serious operations not intervened the manuscript might have been longer, for several written lists still exist of people and events she presumably had intended to include.' (This reminds us all not to leave such things until too late.) 'Tamara said little about her family background. However, memoirs are of little point unless one knows something about the writer and her family: an introductory note was therefore necessary.' This 'introductory note' is a whole family history plus

Tamara Talbot Rice and the cover of her memoirs edited and augmented by her daughter.

Pages from *A Testament to Tennis*, a memoir of her father, by Pru Wallis Myers

family tree, which for me filled in some of the gaps in the Russian side of my family. With footnotes and an epilogue which is an appreciation of Tamara's life and work, plus a bibliography of her published work, her daughter's seamless editing has produced a record of a remarkable life. When asked for a quote in her professional capacity (Elizabeth worked for the National Army Museum, now retired she undertakes military research for historians) she said: 'People do not realise the importance of peripheral material to researchers'. She added, telling several unrepeatable stories of her experiences in such situations: 'Those who research their ancestors must be aware that they may uncover black sheep in the family'.

Tamara, Memoirs of St Petersburg (John Murray 1996) seems a good model for anyone wanting to prepare for publication family material which is of general interest but sorely in need of editing and augmenting. Self-publishing is becoming ever more popular, and easy to manage with computers, scanners and digital cameras there to help. Once you start to plan, whether single handed or as a cooperative project, something worthwhile soon becomes a reality.

Prue Wallis Myers wrote a tribute to her father entitled *A. Wallis Myers, A Tribute to Tennis*. Although this was intended initially for family and friends she had it professionally designed, greatly enhancing its appearance. However, many copies of this book (out of a print run of 300) have gone

Alexander Meadows left a remarkable record of his life, starting with the passenger list from the boat that brought his parents from England in 1884. It provides a vivid and valuable picture of life in Western Australia from the very beginning of the 20th century.

SCHEDULE, 25th VICTORIA, No. 9.

PASSENGER LIST.

to the International Lawn Tennis Club to be distributed – also to the Wimbledon Museum. 'My father was to serve the game of Lawn Tennis all his working life – as a reporter, chronicler, promoter, and in a small but significant way, player. He was tennis correspondent for the *Daily Telegraph* from 1908 to 1938 only interrupted by war service. After the war he was instrumental in the foundation of the International Lawn Tennis Club, founded to avoid fierce competition and instead arrange friendly matches where players from different countries got to know each other. It is prolifically illustrated with photographs of the important players of the day.' The list of her father's publications is impressive and includes *The Complete Lawn Tennis Player* published by Methuen in 1908. As Pru says: 'There is a lot of history in this funny little book'. Many people would agree with the first sentiment but might choose a more impressive adjective instead of the word 'funny'.

People do not always realise the value of their own, or their ancestor's memoirs. At a small bed and breakfast establishment, in a rather remote part of Western Australia, I was shown a memoir written by the grandfather of my hostess, Alexander Meadows (1891–1988). Like many proud Australians it began with the ship's 1884 passenger list which included the name of his mother. His earliest memories were of standing on the verandah of his then West Perth house and watching the camel teams go by on their way to the Kalgoorlie gold fields with all kinds of merchandise: 'There would be six teams of six camels in each team and a man in charge of each

team walking beside them, while the owner leading them, riding a camel'. His next memory, aged about four years old, was driving down the sandy track in his grandfather's spring cart to Subiaco, where they were building a new house, only the twelfth house to be built there. Subiaco is now one of the most prosperous suburbs of Perth. He followed his mother into the Mormon Church and wrote an account entitled: 'Some Early History of the Church here in Western Australia'. All this and detailed reports of his schooling and of his varied work in a foundry, on the railways (in 1909) and in charcoal burning, market gardening and forestry amongst other things, paint a vivid picture of the early development of Perth. I can only hope that they acted on my suggestion and donated a copy to the State Library.

Researching the history of a family house can be an interesting project. This one was published in an archeological magazine. The illustrations are by architect, Nicholas Rose.

Memoirs (also diaries or letters) can be rewritten into a fictional form. The series of six books written by Laura Ingalls Wilder about her pioneering childhood, starting with *The Little House in the Big Woods*, springs to mind. A further manuscript was found after her death. It was published as *The First Four Years*. (Harper and Row 1971). It tells of the start of her married life: 'Just as she wrote it down in pencil, in an orange covered notebook many years ago.' This includes an epilogue by her daughter, where photographs of the main characters allow reality to break through to augment imagination. This vivid chronicle is completed by *West from Home* (Harper and Rose 1974), a volume of her letters edited by Roger Lea MacBride. He wrote: 'Tumbled in a cardboard box along with old recipes, faded pictures, and newspaper clippings of persons and events long gone, I found these letters and postcards from Laura Ingalls Wilder to her husband, Alamanzo'. There is even an appendix, an article (condensed), published in 1915 in the *Missouri Ruralist*, entitled, 'Magic in Plain Food'. It consists of a mix of recipes from all over the world from the Food Products Building in the San Francisco Exposition. This varied collection of books is a most satisfying use of both memoirs and memorabilia.

A collection of memoirs on the same theme or concerning the same moment in time, complement each other, and would compound their value in the eyes of social historians. Memory is such a selective, personal matter so to get short memoirs from three sisters (my aunts) is particularly revealing. The eldest called hers 'My Anecdotage'. Her headings include A Few Short Lives, Coincidences and a Few Little Oddities. Among more serious matters, such as descriptions of poverty in the streets of London after the Boer War, she related one of the family's favourite stories. It concerns my grandfather's Welsh cook's grey African parrot, Bobby. 'It was during the war of 1939-45 that he began to forecast the Derby winner – or at least to choose the winner's name

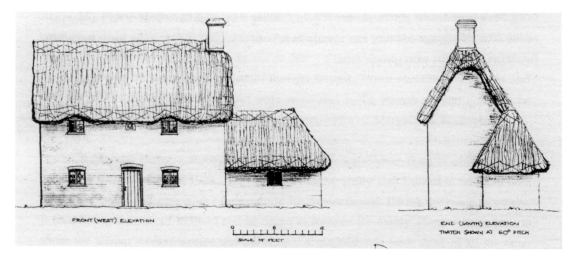

FRONT (WEST) ELEVATION

SCALE OF FEET

END (SOUTH) ELEVATION
THATCH SHOWN AT 60° PITCH

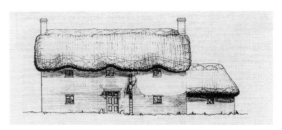

written and rolled up indistinguishable from those of all other starters – often twenty of them. About twenty-four hours before the race this was done with his owner and others looking on. For either four or, I rather think, five years running he got it right. This leaked out and all sorts of people telephoned to find out Bobby's choice. My father was very upset, not wishing to be involved in this. At last, to his relief, Bobby chose wrong and the whole performance lapsed.'

Something included in her memoirs opens yet another aspect of chronicle keeping. It concerns the history of an old cottage that was her home for many years. Entitled *A Very Ordinary Village House, See How They Grow*. Illustrated by the architect Nicholas Rose, it was published in the *Wiltshire Archaelogical and Natural History Magazine*.

My middle aunt preferred to keep a voluminous scrapbook concerning the family. She was more interested in the social side of life. Everything she considered important was carefully documented with photographs and newspaper cuttings.

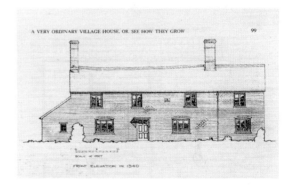

My youngest aunt wrote a more extensive memoir. First she described in great detail, every room in her parent's house. She told of the furniture and ornaments in each room, and what had become of some of these as they have been handed down through several subsequent generations. She even noted the newspapers that were delivered (including *Rainbow* and *Tiger Tim* for herself) and the shops they frequented for various items. Then she wrote a section of what she termed 'sketches' of all her uncles and aunts

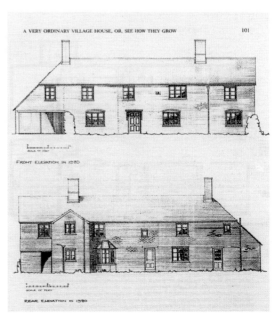

which brings a whole generation to life for those of us who might have just known one or two of them in extreme old age.

One of the happenings that both these last two sisters referred to was perhaps more of general interest – a bit about their uncle Alec who married Charles Dicken's granddaughter – how he had a stage built for his wife to play her violin, and for the Dickens family to produce playlets. This is enlarged on by my youngest aunt: 'Where I came into this was as an "actress". Mrs Henry Dickens wrote plays for children and members of the Dickens family of all ages took part. In one particular play Doris and Monica Dickens took part as two little birds. (She could even recall the song they sang.) One of my cousins was a moth and I was a bat. This play later outgrew the small stage and was transferred to the Lyric Theatre, Hammersmith.'

When searching through her sister's scrapbook there, to wind up the story, was a photograph (undated) titled 'Great Grandchildren of Dickens'. The caption reads: 'There are nine of them and they are all taking part in Rainbowland, a fairy-tale for little folk composed by Mrs H C Dickens, and

GREAT-GRANDCHILDREN OF DICKENS

There are nine of them, and they are all taking part in "Rainbowland," a fairy-play for little folk, composed by Mrs. H. C. Dickens, and performed at Royal Court Theatre matinées.

Opposite: A nineteenth century painting of this family kitchen is so accurate that it allows descendents to spot

some of the possessions that have been handed down over the generations.

Opposite below: A photograph of some of Dickens's descendants, from a family scrapbook.

What a pity the album of cuttings r invitations has been ransacked. It would have been a wonderful historic document — I only wish I had thought to make something similar

performed at Royal Court Theatre matinées' (some discrepancy there.).

This all goes to show how short memoirs, when combined, bring the characters in a family and their environment into sharper focus. Obituaries or eulogies may add yet another, perhaps outside perspective.

How often, even within a close family, when it is too late, we wish that we had listened more carefully or someone had questioned the older generation on any number of subjects and recorded their answers in some way. A Hungarian woman wrote of her childhood c.1914: 'Our grandfather could sit for hours on the terrace overlooking the lake, a long pipe in his mouth obviously enjoying the enchanting view of Lake Balaton surrounded by vineyards', She related how her grandfather remembered various episodes from the family's illustrious past. He wanted her and her brothers to know and remember them too. 'Alas, we were too young to appreciate these precious historical anecdotes

Never think that any record of a life is irrelevant. It is the words of ordinary people, not only the rich and famous, that illuminate our past.

and took greater interest in the two crowns our grandmother gave us to buy a souvenir in the local shops'.

To many people a much loved voice would be even more evocative than the written trace. It is really quite simple today. Most homes have access to some means of recording – the simpler and more unobtrusive the better. With a little persuasion, those who might be reluctant, or even unable, to put pen to paper might be willing to talk about the conditions of their childhood, for instance or other interesting moments in their lives. As someone said to me: 'Record now, by whatever means, while contemporaries are alive, or wait and ponder.' In what other visual ways can you bring your ancestors to life, other than the obvious solution of using photographs? What about drawings or even better cartoons that are even more revealing than portraits – even though this is stretching the subject of this book a bit?

Professionally, the gathering and recording of oral history has become a valuable part of the work of archivists, social historians and other

In your quest for 'voices' from the past do not neglect to record your own memoirs. They will be just as valued by future generations.

Drawings, such as this cutting from an undated newspaper of a distant relative's wedding dress add atmosphere to a memoir.

This is the Beautiful Wedding Gown Made for Miss Gladys Waley.

researchers. One archivist, involved in such work said: 'Most working people do not write or record their experiences having neither the time, resources nor perhaps the confidence that their life stories offer significant and important insights into our society. These experiences need to be recorded now as the voices of the underclass is so often silent. We need to keep all levels, not only the top level. We need everyday experiences.'

What about the value of such things to the writer? Reminiscence writing is a well-known therapy for the elderly in retirement homes. When the person concerned is unable or unwilling to write anything down, their memories can be recorded and scribed by someone else. They can refresh memories, provoke lively discussion between those of a similar age, and perhaps, most important, enhance the self esteem and confidence of those who think their past experiences are worthless and of no interest to younger generations of today. Asking the elderly to think back 50 years or so, to reminisce on such subjects as shops, food, and clothes or perhaps Sundays or public transport, can be as stimulating as it is therapeutic.

I was told: 'Those responsible for rest homes could encourage their residents to have reminiscence sessions – and the time would pass more pleasantly for those folk who spend silent hours lining the walls of sitting rooms between meals. The idea has been taken on successfully (though not without problems) in many sheltered homes; it requires enterprise and patience among the nurses and visitors but can produce fascinating reminiscences of the not-too-distant past.' It is a way of breaking into the shell of isolation that imprisons many of our elderly citizens, and can be a bridge between them and the next generation (or two) who may be avid for the fascinating details locked into the memories of grandparents and others.

Cartoons, such as this one from a nineteenth century issue of *Vanity Fair*, or the early twentieth century silhouette, can sometimes suggest more than a simple faded photograph or formal portrait.

Before we leave the subject of memoirs it should be put into a wider geographic perspective – away from the family tree. Several years ago I was asked to give a workshop on Keeping Chronicles to a group of women from overseas. When looked at in this context, memoirs took on other functions. First was the importance of them to developing countries, not only in the Commonwealth but worldwide. Anything documenting a struggle for freedom could form the basis for the history of an evolving nation. Yet first-hand records of such political or military struggles (from the angle of a freedom fighter and not distorted by hindsight) would be few and far between owing to the very situation prevailing at such a time.

When asked to give an example of how chronicles might be used in their work, few of the group replied. It seemed as if they did not consider such matters important so concerned were they in their day to day endeavours in their own countries. It needed a different question to provoke a discussion – 'What do you most regret not chronicling in your own life and work?' Then, for example, they could see the vital importance of chronicles perhaps to preserve some of the aspects of their fast disappearing culture – crafts, festival, traditional recipes or remedies. The list is endless. What about using such chronicles as relevant literacy material for the next generation? It would fulfil a double purpose. If one person's memories are not enough an anthology could easily be compiled. In this way and many others the concept of the value of memoirs can be enhanced.

P&O

AND

BRITISH INDIA

Steam Navigation Companies

List of Passengers by

P. & O. s.s. "MALOJA."

Leaving LONDON – 13th January, 1933
Leaving MARSEILLES 20th January, 1933.

PASSENGER OFFICES.

P & O HOUSE, 14, COCKSPUR St., LONDON, S.W.1
F. H. GROSVENOR, MANAGER

Strand Passenger Office, AUSTRALIA HOUSE, W.C. 2.
City Passenger Office, 130, LEADENHALL St., E.C. 3.
General Offices, 122, LEADENHALL St., LONDON, E.C. 3.

QUIS SEPARABIT

CHAPTER 6

Travel records

A photographic record is what is often considered the best (and easiest) way of preserving the memory of an exciting voyage. A visual record undoubtedly does just that – records a certain scene or group of people at a certain location. This has special meaning for the photographer and perhaps those who were present. The pleasure that such a record gives to those individuals is not to be underestimated. Taking a photograph of a scene, however, often means that anything out of the picture may be ignored or forgotten. A written record may also be selective, but usually deals with a broader picture and issues that tend to be of increasing general interest in future years, but how many people keep such records today?

On an academic trip that wandered all over China in the early 1980s I met a young man who spent every evening writing up a detailed diary. He said that he was inspired by a much treasured record of travels made by one of his ancestors and wanted to leave a similar record for his family in the future. I regret that I have only a photographic record and hazy memories of many details – however, I treasure the picture of the beautiful ceramic rubbish bins that were everywhere but had disappeared and been replaced by plastic ones by the time of my next visit. Is that symbolic of progress?

On my book shelves is a volume that reminds me of the relaxed accounts of interesting voyages that came out not so long ago. That was before the advent of the celebrity trips that hit the shelves and screens. Today, travel journalism is a profession and your journey would have to be pretty spectacular to

A soon-to-disappear ceramic rubbish bin, Beijing 1985.

The cover of the published account of two young men's journey along the length of the Americas in the early 1960s.

Below: The type of Air France flying boat that took the Lewis-Barneds on part of their journey to India in 1934.

interest a publisher. In the early 1960s two young men joined an expedition to travel the length of the continent from the southernmost tip of South America to Alaska and the Arctic Circle. According to the fly leaf, Mike Andrews was recruited as photographer 'with a hopeful eye on his ability to make money', and Ben Mackworth-Praed as a mechanic to keep the Land Rover and trailer together on what they said 'masqueraded as roads'. It was called The Year with Three Summers, published by Cassell & Company Ltd. Maybe the book did not have a huge readership, but what a record to leave for subsequent generations of their families.

Major Lewis-Barned and his wife both left amusing accounts of their journey to India by air, in 1934. It forms part of a family history compiled by their son. They were returning after home leave. The journey took five days. They travelled partly by a small flying boat from Marseilles stopping at Bastia on Corsica to refuel, then Naples again to refuel and finally to Corfu where they spent the night. Some of their comments make it seem miraculous that anyone survived. 'It was a very small flying boat, carrying only a maximum of four passengers and a crew of three: mechanic, wireless operator and pilot. (Later they described how all three took it in turns to fly the machine although only the pilot was qualified.) 'This machine had two engines, one behind another, and it was necessary to climb an almost vertical ladder and then descend through the pilot's cockpit, into the passenger cabin. It was

A sketch of one of their Indian homes by Dorothy Lewis Barned reproduced from a family history compiled by their son.

Below: A magnificently simplified map of Ceylon from a 1930s account of a round-the-world trip.

8 BRUNTON RD   BANGALORE

divided by a glass door through which we were able to see the crew smoking all through the journey, although we were not allowed to. The windows were like port holes, which we only discovered on the second day that it was possible to open. One had to be careful to keep them tightly shut when landing and taking off otherwise a deluge came in .... It was amusing to watch the mechanics washing their hands in the petrol which was being fed into the tanks of the machine. We hoped that none of the dirt would be fed into the carburettor.'

The next day in Athens, they reported that they had a smoke on the top of the plane while it was refuelling! By the fourth day they were back in a 'high winged monoplane' for the rest of their journey. Mrs Lewis-Barned was a talented artist and left a series of drawings and paintings that documented their life in India and are much treasured by their descendents (and, incidentally, merited a proper exhibition when discovered, hidden under her bed, in extreme old age).

Another journey also in the early 1930s, this time around the world, is chronicled by one of my aunts. The copious photographs, the carefully typed account and the other memorabilia brings vividly to mind the atmosphere, as well as some of the perceptions of a bygone age of travel. In Burma she wrote: 'The people vary enormously, and it was interesting to see the different types

SOUVENIR OF THE SLOTTED WING
AVRO - AVAIN
"CANBERRA PUP"

VH - UIV

AS USED BY BERT HINKLER

wearing the most picturesque clothes – only rather a shock to find an occasional one in brightly coloured silks complete with a Homburg hat, riding a bicycle…. The Irrawaddy was very shallow at this time of year and full of sandbanks. These native villages make me think of the exhibition villages at Wembley – each house raised several feet from the ground on posts – one cannot help feeling that they have been specially arranged there for our amusement.'

Later: 'We reached the Equator on Saturday night on the Op Ten Oort. I sat between an American whose main ambition seemed to be to end his days in Mexico City, and a Dutchman who kept repeating that if the British could only learn a few lessons from the Dutch, they wouldn't now be on the point of losing India – we reached Batavia at dawn.'

Our Australian grandchildren should find the descriptions of their country and of distant relations nearly a century ago, interesting one day. It shows how little people knew then about life on the other side of the world. It was obviously a huge education for this rather sheltered Londoner. After a visit to a large sheep station called Widgiewa on the borders of Victoria, in the middle of winter and a severe drought, she wrote: 'This week has been a complete eye-opener for me. I had no idea that any country life could be so utterly different from ours. There is nothing to see but brown grass and the occasional dead tree.' And then:

The contents of this large album have remained in good condition partly because nothing was stuck down – photos, typewritten text and memorabilia were all kept in place with old-fashioned photo adhesive corners.

'Australians consider the Jenolam Caves one of the sights of the world but what amused me far more were the wallabies which are so tame that I was able to take several snap shots of them feeding out of Cecile's hands.'

Cecile. Was she dressed like this to feed the Wallabies?

So, what might constitute a travel record other than photographs or a full written account? It would depend on the tastes and character of the traveller. One person might find memorabilia such as the passenger list from a cruise ship the most important thing to keep. For another annotated maps would be preferable.

More excerpts from the 'round-the-world' trip.

ORIENT LINE

PASSENGER LIST

Some reminders of a trip
from Uganda through
what was then the
Belgian Congo in 1960.

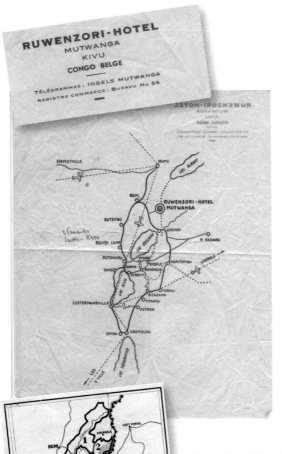

I was looking through some of my late mother's papers when I found the few things that she had kept from a trip we took her on – round the western Congo (Belgian as it was then) – when she came to visit us in Uganda in late 1959. I came across a map,that had been printed on the back of the flimsy airmail stationery from the rest house where we stayed. It showed how to reach this out of the way place in the middle of what was then the Albert National Park. That, along with another map of the park, mentioned places that surely no longer exist as tourist venues. The names of Kivu and Kisenyi are now synonymous with war and destruction. The park is unlikely to have survived in its original form. Who knows, they may be of historical interest one day – only because they are the kind of thing that other people throw away.

Our children were encouraged to keep holiday books from an early age. Today, they are some of their most treasured possessions. These diaries are augmented by drawings, advertisements,

All that remains to remind one daughter of a journey through Tibet. Her written account and carefully preserved letters were stolen once back in London.

food wrappings, tickets and of course postcards and maps. There is little of general interest except perhaps an account of a major tanker spill which devastated the beaches of Brittany in 1969, with maps and cuttings from the local paper. Erquy came forever to be known in the family as Murky Erquy.

All three daughters continued this habit into student days. Their travel journals were not intended for publication, in the way that many people today undertake unusual journeys with a book or television film in mind. However one

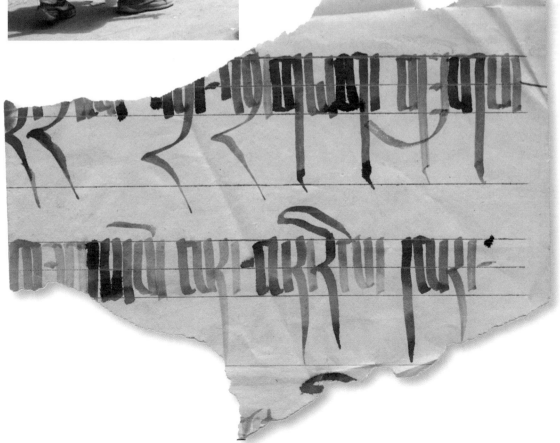

daughter's account of a summer spent with Sami reindeer herders in Lappland did get published in her university journal. It is another daughter's journey into Tibet just as the monasteries were being destroyed that is more relevant here. Her records were stolen while she was moving house and little remains now. I had borrowed some photographs that were used in a book about writing systems, one was used on the cover. What also remains, because I had borrowed them to use as illustrations, are fragments of the monks' and their students' writing. She rescued them from a monastery fire that was meant to destroy everything. In a way those fragments catch that moment in history more vividly than any photograph.

> Few people would consider that the raw material of their travels – plane or boat tickets, hotel bills with airline or luggage labels worth keeping. Yet they would make a satisfying record that like any collection becomes more fascinating to the collector or following generations the longer they are kept.

My husband has kept records of our early family holidays. One letter is dated 7th March 1962 from Four Seasons Travel. It read: 'We have today received from the Pension Rustique an offer for your holiday. The charges are 20 New Francs (approximately 13 N F to the pound sterling) per day an adult, children pay half price. Monsieur Marie writes that a young person can be found to look after the children, equally a blanchiseuse for the nappies and for other washings will be at your disposal. The cost of these extra services are not included in the twenty francs but it will not amount to very much since in Brittany exist still relics of the paternalistic society and looking after children and washing is regarded as the duty of the daughter.' (Now I recollect that the travel agent was Hungarian hence the rather strange wording.)

Attached to the sheaf of papers is an important looking letter from the Consulat General de France printed in purple ink stating the following: 'All persons entering France should be the holder of an international certificate of vaccination against smallpox dated less than three years (underlined)'. This would be quite enough to put me off the holiday but, typed in black at the bottom of the page appeared this inexplicable message: 'NB These regulations only apply to persons from the district of Rhondda and Llantrisant, Glamorganshire'. Had there been an outbreak of smallpox in Wales in 1962?

At the end of a careful sheet of accounts appears: 'Cost in France excluding travel but including everything else: £9 per day of which hotel £5 per day'. This was for four of us and the food was wonderful even if the Salle a Manger consisted of a long table in the orchard.

Our next French holiday is commemorated by the ticket and boarding card of a trip from Lympne to Montpelier by Skyways Coach Air Ltd. By having the return ticket, unused, I am suddenly reminded of a fearsome train journey standing all day jammed in a corridor, with two children

Tickets and a record of
expenses are reminders
of a 1960s trip to Brittany.

under five years old, because there was a strike of some sort. Incidentally, the children survived on a diet of peaches that we had intended to bring back as presents and thought it all a huge adventure. There is nothing to remind me of how we eventually got back to England. I can only remember an altercation at midnight on a Paris station as we tried to contact the agents.

How you record a journey and what you choose to retain remains a very personal matter. How interesting or valuable it will be to anyone in the future other than the traveller is very much a matter of chance. Some of the records may be useful for comparison with a similar journey years,

or generations later. Some may astound you with their modest cost, if you have kept accounts, while others may prove important by documenting places that have since been obliterated or happenings that otherwise might not have been chronicled. All that it is possible to say is that if you do not keep that record some day you may regret it.

No 2275

Fire Rigsdaler.

Hartmann
1760.

Jøden Moses Marcus Melchior
og hans forr, ... at man
... dig i Kiøbenhavn
... hans ... ...
... ...
Nathan ... ...,
... at ... 100 Rd til Politie
Cassen. ——

Dateret Christiansborg Slot d: 27de
Martii A:o 1760.

CHAPTER 7

Business and legal records

The term 'business records' suggests pages of figures, and that is what is most important to many people, but there are many other aspects that reflect the history and progress of an enterprise. Some companies employ archivists and keep copious records and memorabilia while others, in these days of mergers and takeovers, lose their archives – if ever they existed.

The history of a business can make interesting reading. An example of what can be done with documents and other memorabilia is a book that was privately published by a firm of Danish merchants. All that appears on the cover are the dates 1761–1961, and inside: *Six Generations of a Merchant Dynasty*. On the first page there is a reproduction of the firm's permit to trade. There is a beautifully scribed list dated 1768 which suggests that such papers were carefully preserved. It provides a record of how each generation expanded the business, starting with: 'Foreign goods, such as leather and tobacco'. The next generation: 'Greatly extended the scope which included the import of cane sugar and rum from the then Danish West Indies'. They opened branches as far away as Melbourne and, again, that mention of the Danish West Indies. In the nineteenth century they became Denmark's leading tea importers: 'When the first tea clippers of the season were expected in London, the heads of the house used to travel there to make their purchases at the tea-auctions in Mincing Lane'. In the early twentieth century one of the first innovations was: 'To import

A permit to trade dated January 7 1761 and a painting of one of their clipper ships. From *Six Generations of a Merchant Dynasty*, a record of the Melchior family firm.

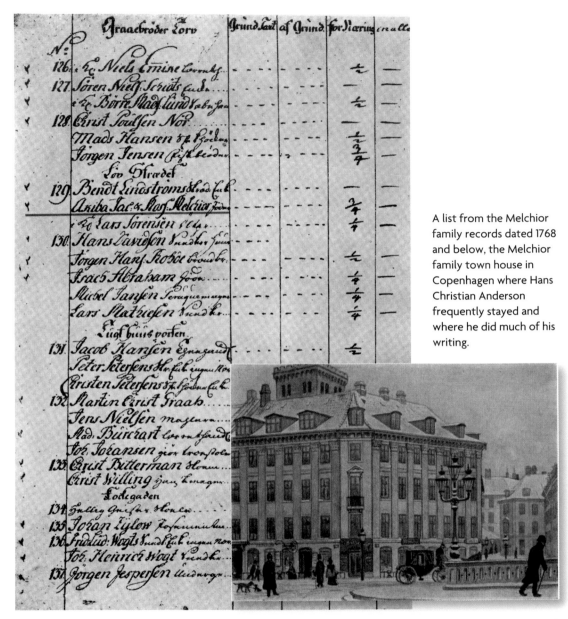

A list from the Melchior family records dated 1768 and below, the Melchior family town house in Copenhagen where Hans Christian Anderson frequently stayed and where he did much of his writing.

green coffee, which has since become the main commodity of the firm.'

As well as the obligatory portraits of each generation of the Melchior family, and descriptions of their interests outside the business, there is a reproduction of a painting of their home as it was in the nineteenth century. There are also illustrations of some of the ships that carried the commodities they dealt in. The family firm has now ceased trading but this record remains to pass on to future generations. It gives a satisfying picture of a time when merchandise was shipped from all over the world in the company's fleet of sailing and steam vessels, and would serve as a model for others who might wish to do likewise. Enterprises do not necessarily have to be old to be worthwhile recording – they will become history soon enough.

Old bills are reminders of shops that
no longer exist and, when dated, tell of
prices as they were many years ago.

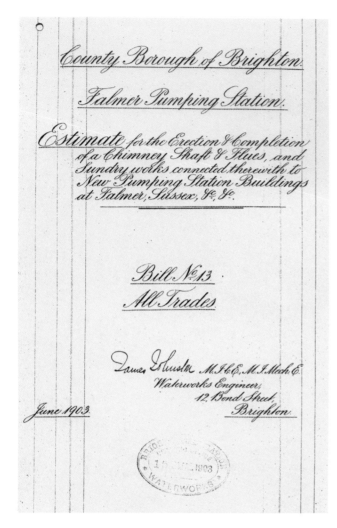

Bills alone make a meaningful and decorative collection. A craft shop near my home took over an old established village grocer and found in some nook or cranny of the building a cache of bills dating back several centuries. These they had framed and used as an effective decoration – rather appropriate as it happens for their new enterprise which always put an emphasis on calligraphy. Bills in general (provided they are dated) reveal the prices and details of goods or services when certain of our ancestors paid for them. Their decorative letter headings are a record of family shops that have long disappeared from our high streets. Bills from

Bills reflect many different aspects, such as the skill of the handwriting and presentation as in this engineers report dated 1903, and Waterlow's invoice from the 1850s, or informative, as in this extensive list of the teas from J Lyons in 1922.

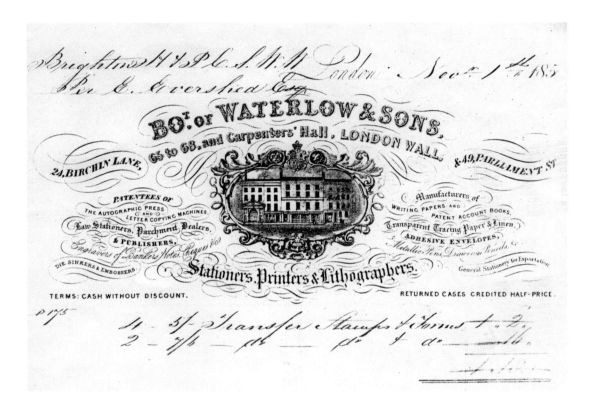

individual tradesmen reveal how plumbers, carpenters and others who practised their day-to-day skills in the community reached a high standard of handwriting that would put their present-day counterparts to shame.

It is not, however, only decorative bills or receipts that are interesting. A set of rather dull looking ones hide a story of how one man saved some scraps of history from being lost. Port Augusta is in South Australia. It used to be a thriving port, supplying all kinds of goods and supplies for the hinterland and exporting wool and other products. Now the waterfront is a sad, almost derelict place. A few years ago the old

custom house was being bulldozed and burned when Mr Whiting happened to pass by. He managed to rescue several volumes and other torn sheets containing irreplaceable records from the custom house, and bonded warehouse. Some of them need an explanation – the crosses instead of signatures belong to the Afghan camel drivers who loaded and transported goods to the interior.

Mr Whiting was obviously aware of the importance of keeping all kinds of records, and his memorabilia would be welcomed by any reference library, record office or museum. He gave me a fragment of an article that recorded ships of the fleet, the ship's company and the

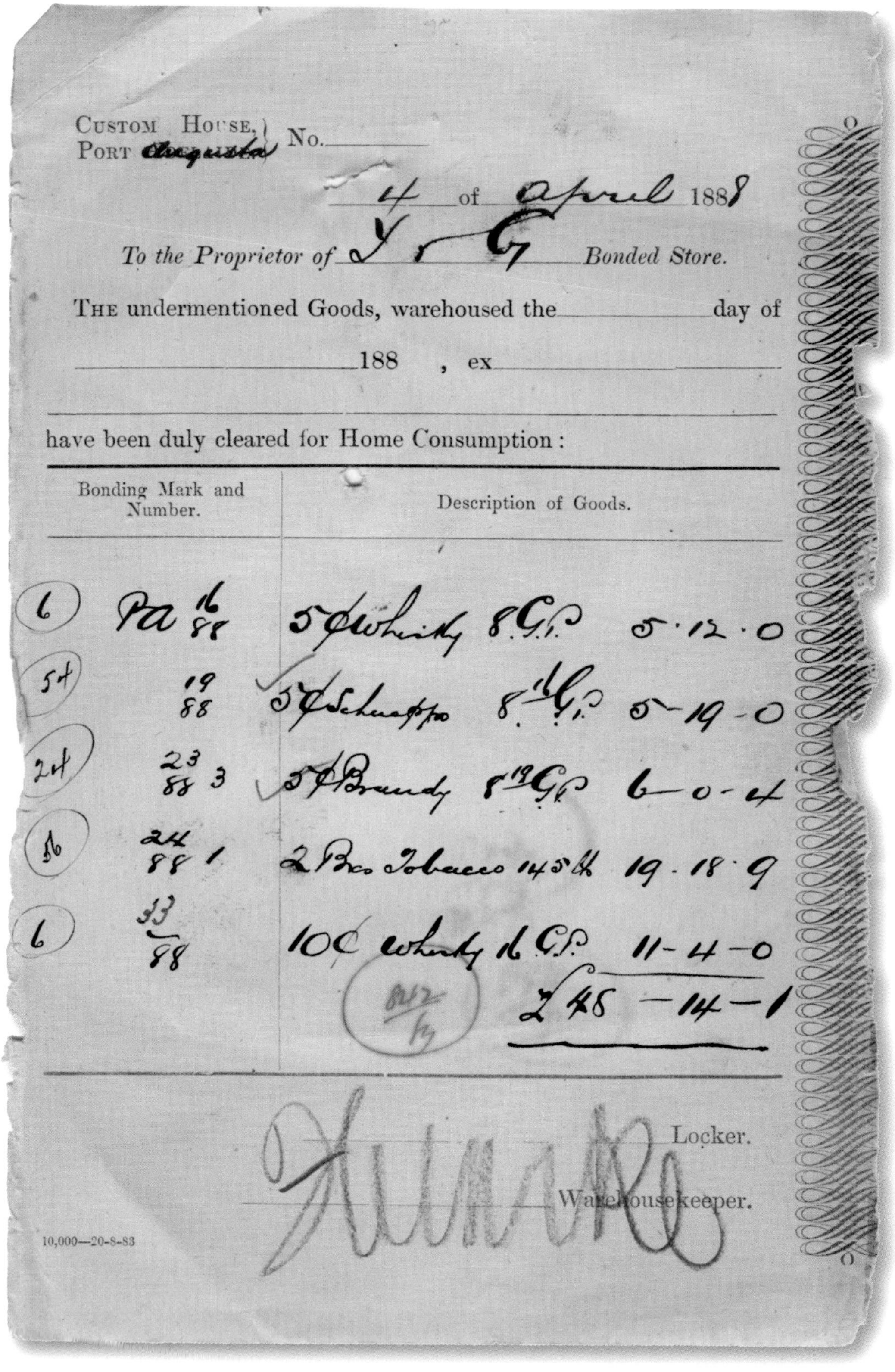

CUSTOM HOUSE,⎫
PORT *Augusta* ⎬ No._____

4 of *April* 188*8*

To the Proprietor of *J G* Bonded Store.

THE undermentioned Goods, warehoused the_____ day of

_____ 188 , ex_____

have been duly cleared for Home Consumption :

Bonding Mark and Number.	Description of Goods.	
⑥ PA 16/88	5 q Whisky 8.G.P.	5 · 12 · 0
54 19/88	5 q Schnapps 8 G.P.	5 - 19 - 0
24 23/88 3	5 q Brandy 8 G.P.	6 - 0 - 4
56 24/88 1	2 Bxs Tobacco 145 lb	19 · 18 · 9
⑥ 53/88	10 q Whisky 1. G.P.	11 - 4 - 0
		£ 48 - 14 - 1

_____ Locker.

_____ Warehousekeeper.

10,000—20-8-83

These invoices were rescued when Port Augusta's custom house in South Australia was being destroyed. They reveal how produce was shipped in and out of the port carried by Afghan camel traders, and how they signed their names. Mr Whiting, who saved these documents, also had kept the cutting that reported his convict ancestor's crime, and other memorabilia that showed how his descendent had prospered in the years ahead.

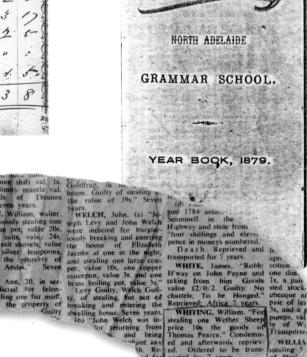

prisoners who had been transported. Unfortunately it is not dated, but it gave details of their crimes and their sentences. There possibly is his ancestor, William Whiting: 'For stealing one Wether Sheep price 10s the goods of Thomas Pearce. Condemned and afterwards reprieved. Ordered to be transported for 7 years.' William's descendants must have done well because I was also given a copy of the North Adelaide Grammar School's year book dated 1879, with the name W E Whiting.

Old legal documents, indentures, mortgages, leases or conveyances are not only useful in tracing family land purchases or residences but are usually decorative as well. Whether concerned with the family or not, many are worth framing with their beautiful writing penned on vellum in a variety of scripts. I bought the one above for a couple of pounds to show my students when I ran lettering classes, and I know of one person who had her family deeds made into lampshades. They looked impressive in her thatched cottage but that is not at all what this book is about.

The nineteenth century deeds concerning the rather ugly Victorian house where I lived as a child reveal that property deals, division of land and quick profits, were all taking place and the signatures on the documents show that the same families of the solicitors and agents are still around today. One document dated 1882, confirms that Sir John Kirk, who the conveyance tells us was Her Majesty's Consul-General in Zanzibar, was the purchaser. He must have been an eccentric gentleman, bringing back his big game trophies and planting a bamboo grove to house them. By the time we found them, over

This battered indenture, dated April 30 1726, has no family or other connection. It was bought at a time when many such documents were being disposed of very cheaply as offices in London were being redeveloped, and used to illustrate different styles of lettering to calligraphy students.

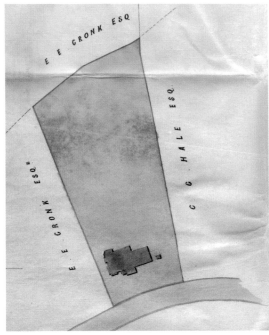

1872

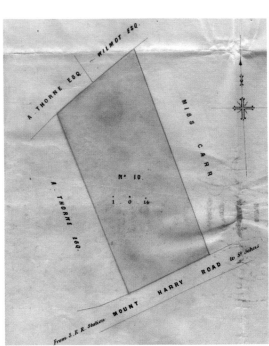

1876

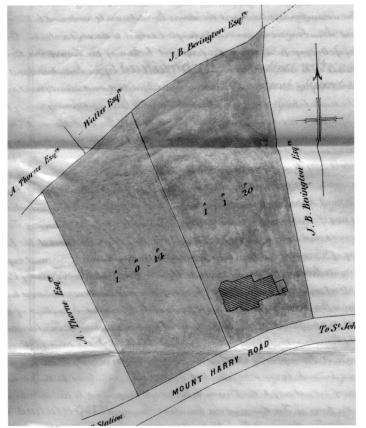

1882

Maps on documents dated between the years 1872 and 1882 tell of the frequent deals and the development of favoured plots of land close to the newly opened Sevenoaks station.

Opposite: The conveyance of the land to Sir John Kirk in 1882. He finally built a house, called Wavertree, after the home of his friend, Lord Lugard in Wavertree, Liverpool.

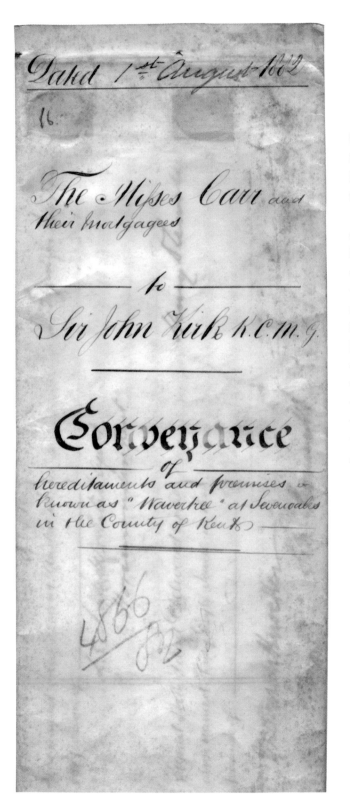

half a century later, they were in the last stages of decay but the buffalo and hippos were exotic play things none the less.

These deeds were accompanied by a carefully researched report on the history of this area and its subsequent development from the Reformation to the present day. It was written by my eldest sister and completed shortly before she died. It records how the land, originally under the Archbishop of Canterbury, reverted to the Crown and was then granted or sold to court favourites or holders of offices under the Crown such as the Sackvilles and Bosvilles. It described those large estates up until the late 1860s when the railway arrived. That opened the possibility of travelling to and from London to work in relative comfort and there became a demand for family houses on the slopes surrounding the main station. That is what led to the development of what my sister termed 'our part of the estate' which was originally the Bosville estate. The deeds tell the rest of the story. This all shows how keeping old deeds and papers, and doing some further research, can result in a record of the development of what is now almost a suburb of London while at the same time revealing part of the family history and providing a fascinating project in retirement.

The advertisement for the sale of Wavertree by Sir John Kirk in 1923. This red brick Victorian house was filled with evacuees during the Second World War and demolished soon after to be replaced by a small block of flats – but the history of it is recorded for the interest of local historians as well as family.

Opposite: valuations for insurance or probate, as well as wills and codicils often disclose useful information for those researching their family history.

BY ORDER OF THE EXECUTORS OF THE LATE SIR JOHN KIRK.   SALE NO. 336.

SEVENOAKS.

Within 10 Minutes walk of the Station, with its 30 Minutes Express Service to the City and West End.

Particulars and Conditions of Sale of the
Substantially-Built Modern

Freehold Residence

KNOWN AS

"Wavertree"

MOUNT HARRY ROAD

Occupying an Elevated Position on Sandy Soil and Enjoying magnificent Views over a wide area of well-wooded and undulating country.

containing :

3 RECEPTION ROOMS   SERVANTS' HALL
GOOD OFFICES   10 BEDROOMS and BATHROOM

PICTURESQUE PLEASURE GROUNDS.

With Rhododendron Walks, fine Specimen and Timber Trees, good Kitchen Garden, &c., in all extending to about

2¼ ACRES

Company's Gas & Water. Main Drainage. Electric Light Available.
VACANT POSSESSION ON COMPLETION.

WHICH

Messrs F. D. IBBETT & Co.

IN CONJUNCTION WITH

Messrs. RALPH PAY & TAYLOR

Are instructed to Sell by Auction,

At the London Auction Mart, 155, Queen Victoria Street, E.C. 4.

On Wednesday, 11th April, 1923

At 2.30 p.m., (unless previously Sold by Private Treaty)

Particulars and Conditions of Sale may be obtained of the Solicitors :
Messrs. Knocker, Knocker & Foskett, Sevenoaks, and of the Auctioneers,
Messrs. Ralph Pay & Taylor, 3, Mount Street, Grosvenor Square, London, W. 1 and
Messrs. F. D. Ibbett & Co., F.A.I., Sevenoaks & Oxted.   Telephone : Sevenoaks 147.

The Caxton Press, High Street, Sevenoaks.

```
Valuation of Silver goods belonging to                    October 1931


No.  Spoons and forks etc.
1.   18 King's pattern Table Spoons  57.5. ozs--------------
     36   "         "         " Forks 119.0  "  --------------
     24   "         "     Dessert Spoons
                                       49.0  "--------------
     18   "         "         " Forks  37.0  "  --------------
     11   "         "     Teaspoons    13.0  "  --------------
     Pr.  "         "     Sauce ladles  6.0.  "  --------------
     "    "         "     Salad Servers10.0  "  --------------        80. -
     1    "         "     Gravy ladle   5.0  "  --------------
     1    "         "     Soup    "    11.5  "  --------------
     1    "         "     Asparagus Tongs
                                        6.1  "  --------------

            314.1 ozs  at approx 5/6 per oz
```

Wills and marriage settlements are more informative still for people researching their family history, as well as those involved in social or perhaps local history, documenting the breakup of estates and transferring of goods, finances or property. It feels like prying into our ancestors private lives to read their bequests and detailed instructions to be carried out after their deaths – but where these valuable (in the sense of family history) documents have been kept maybe it is giving proper recognition to those past generations who have taken such care to preserve them.

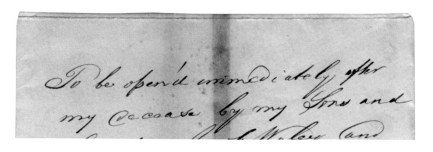

Overleaf: two of the four pages of a Boord family will dated 1663. Patricia Boord writes: 'It is hardly organised at all, but gives a very good and detailed idea of his possessions, those of a yeoman farmer of the time: his furniture, cooking pots, brewing equipment, dairy and farming implements. He does not seem to have owned his farm so his wife can inherit only two shillings and sixpence.'

The fifteenth day of February one thousand six hundred sixty & three, In the name of God Amen I John Board of ye Parish of Killmersdon in ye County of Somset Yeoman being sicke & weake of body but of sound mind & memory blessed by God revoking all former & other Wills by me heretofore made doe now make & ordaine this my last Will & Testament in manner & forme following - First I bequeath my Soul into ye hands of Almighty God my Creator & Jesus Christ my Redeemer by & through whose alone meritts death & pasion I trust & Stedfastly beleive to receive & obtaine everlasting life my body to be buried in ye Churchyard of Kilmersdon aforesaid near ye Little yew tree by ye bodys of my Father & Mother, also I give & bequeath unto my Wife Sarah Board two shillings & six pence in money to be paid her by my Executrix hereafter named Also I give unto my eldest Son Henry Board the bed and bedstead which I now lye uppon also two Blanketts now in ye said bed together wth one Bolster Matt & Cord belonging to ye same & also one arras Coverlidd also I give unto him my said Son Henry all my working tools excepting one handsaw one borier & one wimble, also I give unto my Son Henry aforesaid one Iron Barr & two Iron wedges Also I give unto my Son James one bedstead bedcord & Matt in ye Buttery Chamber & also one bed bolster & two blanketts & one orenge collour Coverlid in ye Chamber over ye kitchen Also I give & bequeath unto my Son Henry one Table board & frame to it also one Cupboard & two formes & two benches allso standing in ye Hall & also one wainscoat chest standing

in ye Chamber I now lye in & near ye door
thereof & also one old chaire in ye Hall &
also these books following viz one book of
Martyrs one book of Mr Cradocks writing one
book of Mr Halls one great bible ye rest of my
books I give to my Son James excepting one
book of Mr Boltons writing Also I give unto my
Son James one Table board & frame to it
together wth one forme one bench one cupboard
all standing in ye Kitchin & also two joint
stools & two chairs standing in ye Kitchin
chimney also I give & bequeath unto my Son
Henry my Brewing furnace with my great
brass pott & ye great hangills & pothooks
belonging to ye same & also my Great Iron
brandiron & my middle brass kettle & also my
bell mettle Skillett & my great Iron spitt &
best brass Scummer & one Iron beef fork also
one other Chaire standing in ye Hall & two
joint stools standing in my Chamber further
I give unto my Son James one great wainscoat
Chest standing in my chamber & also my
second best brass pott with hangills & pothooks
belonging belonging to it & also my biggest
brass kettle & also one little brass Skillett & my
least brass kettle & my least Iron spitt & also
one Timber Silt standing in ye Milkhouse &
also I give to my Son Henry one Cheese wring
standing in ye Milkhouse & also my biggest
barrell with ye horse to carry him & also my
brewing fatt & my best tubb & trendle & also
my two best milking pails & also I give unto
my Son James my next best brewing tubb &
my washing tubb & two lesser barrells & one other
brewing trendle in ye buttery Also I give unto my
daughter Elizabeth May The bedsteed bed bolster two

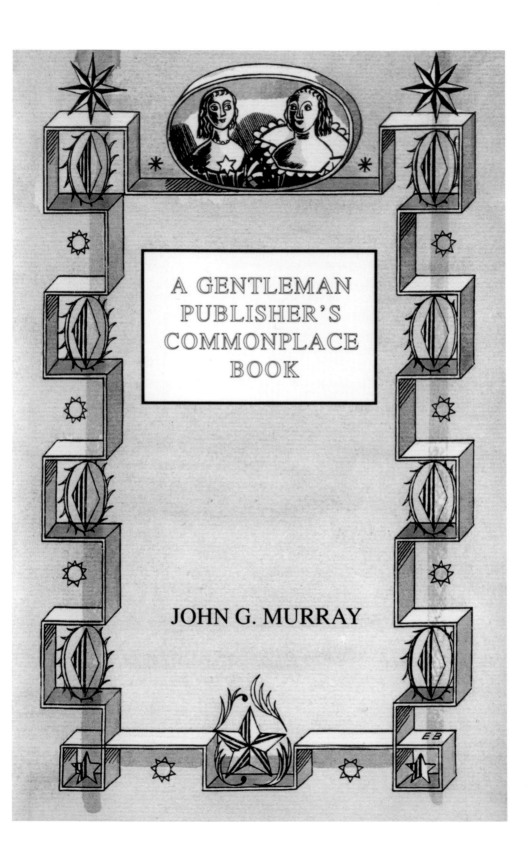

A GENTLEMAN PUBLISHER'S COMMONPLACE BOOK

JOHN G. MURRAY

CHAPTER 8

Day books, commonplace books and albums

Whether you refer to such personal anthologies as day books or commonplace books or whatever, an original manuscript of this sort written by someone in the family or acquired in some way, is to be treasured. Some older ones are so interesting that they merit being produced as facsimiles, where the beauty of their calligraphy combines with the fascination of their contents. Being as they are, personal, their variability depends on the tastes and occupation and perhaps the age of the compiler, and perhaps the usage intended.

The older they are the more books reflect the times that they were written, in their choice of material. In the past they might have consisted of a collection of recipes, remedies and perhaps folklore. These can reveal beliefs that may appear unusual today. It was a popular occupation for all ages in the nineteenth century in particular, and there must be many well loved compilations preserved by families today, Goodly tracts played a prominent part, as well as favourite proverbs, sayings or poems, and occasionally illustrations. In later years the contents became more light-hearted. Some included contributions by friends or relatives, becoming precursors of the somewhat sentimental autograph albums of the early twentieth century.

A Gentleman Publisher's Commonplace Book by John G Murray brings this genre into the present day. His son, John R Murray, published a selection in 1996, explaining: 'Whenever he came across something wise, thoughtful, inspiring, witty or simply odd he would write it into a tiny blue notebook he kept in his inside jacket pocket and then, when he had time, decant it into the commonplace book proper'. This meant that if he had to give a speech; 'He would always dip into his commonplace book and draw out the perfect proverb or saying for the occasion'.

Those that I have acquired or had access to through friends, are the work of ordinary people

The cover of this selection from John G Murray's commonplace book, compiled by his son, and published in 1996, shows that this tradition survived well into the modern age.

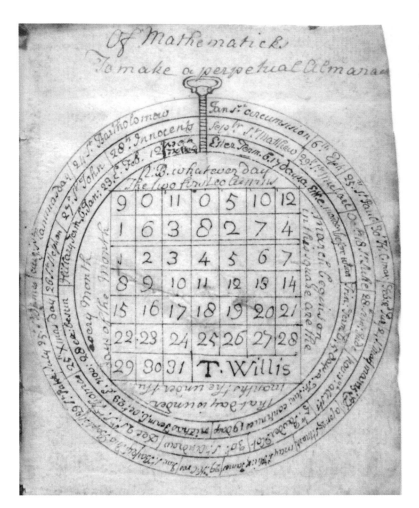

How to make a perpetual almanac, from Thomas Willis – his book, age 14 years, dated 25th December 1745.

– not important personages. Catherine Draper's family has one such treasure that has been handed down through successive generations since it was written by a young man in 1745. It would be memorable for its tiny and precise handwriting if nothing else as the vellum bound volume is small enough to be held in the palm of one hand. However, the contents and illustrations mark it out as something special. The first page proclaims its impressive title: 'Youth's General Instructor or a Short and Easy Introduction to Some Diverting and Useful Arts and Sciences by Thomas Willis'. The next page presents a slightly different idea of the writer; the contents are a mixture reflecting an unusual youth's various

interests. Sadly, when he died at the age of 24, little was known about him in the family. This is the only reminder of his life. The first section, headed: 'For painting' consists mostly of instructions on how to grind pigments and obtain certain colours. His interest in such matters and artistic inclinations are demonstrated in no uncertain manner by the few illustrations. Later entries betray his youth or fantasies. How to make a sparrow white is a particularly nasty inclusion: 'When it is young pull its feathers till you see them come white then let them grow'. 'How to make the figure of a man grow in a mandrake' is another. But more interesting as an indication of the age he lived in is his paragraph

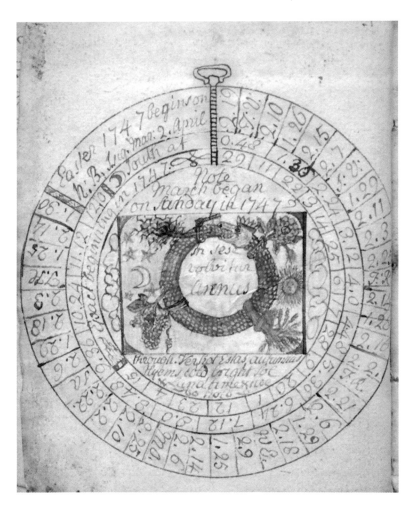

entitled 'Electricity'. Somewhat enigmatically this relates: 'A stick of sealing wax or brimstone rubbed against woollen will attract. Paper, snapfire and spirit of wine also a table of glass will perform the value.' The most decorative pages are those where he produced a design for a 'perpetual almanack'.

The loan of this book led to an interesting trip to our county archive at Canterbury to consult the archivist about its preservation. Her advice was to guard against the hidden cause of cumulative damage caused by storage. As a result an acid free box is being made to fit. The small book was in good condition – only care had to be taken when turning the pages for perusal or

photography, but the advice about the conservation of other family books or manuscripts was very practical. It was that you should keep anything, however damaged, and however expensive its restoration might be. Someone further down the line might spend the money necessary to restore it – this was in reference to a damaged family Bible that would be costly to restore.

I found several very different examples of the genre of day or commonplace books in the collection of copybooks discussed later on. In 1820, to be precise on the 17th August, in Sandgate, the Rev Bartlet Goodrich started such a book with dated entries on serious and uplifting

The first page of a book written by Reverend Bartlet Goodrich dated 17th August 1820. The second page, reflecting the contents, begins: 'On transcribing Mr Locke's recommendations as a motto for this book, the doubt immediately suggested itself whether my most valuable thoughts would repay the trouble of committing them to paper, or any future reader that of their perusal'.

Rev.d Bartlet Goodrich.

1820.

"Never go without a pen and ink, or something, to write down all thoughts of moment that come into your mind – I must own I have often omitted it, and have often repented of it. The thoughts that come unsought, and, as it were, drop into the mind, are commonly the most valuable of any we have, and therefore should be secured, because they seldom return –" Locke –

. Sandgate 17th Aug.t

subjects as befitting his calling. On the first page he copied out an appropriate paragraph written by the philosopher John Locke (1632–1704): 'Never go without a pen and ink, or something, to write down all the thoughts that come into your mind – I must own I have often omitted it, and have often repented of it. The thoughts that come unsought, and as it were, drop into the mind, are commonly the most valuable of any we have, and therefore should be secured, because they seldom return'.

The Rev Goodrich commences his own efforts thus: 'On transcribing Mr Locke's recommendations as a motto for this book, the doubt immediately suggested itself whether my "most valuable thoughts" would repay the trouble of committing them to paper, or any future reader that of their perusal.' He worried that he would be open to the charge of vanity and ignorance – but not for long. Daily pearls of wisdom flowed from his pen. One week he is asserting: 'A desire for knowledge seems implanted in the human mind. Its sources and means of acquirement may be arranged under the following threefold divisions –

(1) An acquaintance with past events, derived from those sacred and profane records and traditions which preserve them from oblivion.

(2) With the present, – from personal observation or oral and scriptory communications.

(3) With the future, which, excepting those divine revelations it is the will of The Almighty to vouchsafe, must rest solely upon the uncertainty of conjecture, and be regarded as involved in an impenetrable to mortal vision.'

The next week he is observing: 'Among the numerous singularities characteristics of mortal imbecility which, but for the frequency and extent of their predominence would excite astonishment, we may notice a dissatisfied uneasiness in the participation of the present, and inordinate anxiety in regard to the events of futurity.' I fear that his congregations must have suffered many a lengthy sermon based on these themes.

Another volume looks as if it will follow similar lines. It seems to be the property of Mr A Goodrich and dated 1875, despite starting with a poem apparently written by the same Rev B Goodrich and dated 1833. However, on closer inspection, it appears to be a bridge between what we would see as a commonplace book and what would be called today an autograph book, though without illustrations. It includes contributions made over a period of years and is more lighthearted than the clergyman's one, with sayings from Aristotle and the classics to Harriet Beecher Stowe, Victor Hugo and Gladstone and Ella Wheeler Wilcox, among many others. These are penned in several different hands. There are cuttings of whimsical sayings and happenings annoyingly undated. They concern such varied issues as a detailed account of a Shrove Tuesday happening: 'The annual "Pancake greeze" which goes back to a date so remote that its origin is unknown, took place at Westminster School in the presence of all the boys and many of their relatives.' A cutting headed "Biarritz, March 21" tells us that: 'The King took a walk in the streets today and purchased a large number of postcards

The content of a similar type of book by Mr A Goodrich, (maybe the Reverend Bartlet Goodrich's son), dated 1875, consisted of much lighter content. All of these examples come from a collection of books from the Goodrich family covering over a century.

representing incidents in the visit of King Alfonso and Princess Ena of Battenberg.' You could trace the date from that information. Then comes: 'Another interesting item is a humorous letter from Charles Dickens to the sculptor Behnes. The famous novelist had arranged to sit to him for a portrait bust, but failing to keep the appointment despatched the following missive to ward off the sculptor's wrath. The letter started: "Left home on the evening of Tuesday the thirtieth of April a remarkable dog answering to the name of Boz ..."' These cuttings may not do much to illuminate the character of the collector but they make interesting reading.

Tucked into a page at the end of this brown paper covered book (much less imposing than the Rev Bartlet's volume) there is a page from a publication called *The New Idea*, dated 6 June 1907. It looks as if this manuscript was handed down in the family who continued to add to it over many years. Some of the handwriting looks Edwardian, as of course the piece from Biarritz was. Anyhow, that page suggests that contributors may have needed help in selecting suitable poetry from the 'treasuries' submitted by the readers of this

worthy, and what must have been, lengthy book, considering the page is numbered 436.

This idea of collecting sayings and snippets of wisdom is rather strange to young people today. I can remember taking a battered book of quotations along to some lettering classes that I ran a few years ago. It was meant to help students to find something to write out for practise. One young girl became engrossed in reading it and asked in all seriousness where she could find a copy of the book, as if it were the only one rather than an example of a whole multitude of similar anthologies that were popular a century ago, and now can be found on the back shelves of secondhand bookshops.

By the time Rosie Goodrich carried on the family tradition and started her book, as a young schoolgirl in 1888, a few illustrations had started to be included.

Anyhow, it seems as if the tradition has been handed down to a third generation of Goodrichs. Rosie Goodrich started her book in 1888, giving her address as the Convent School, Oxford. Her tastes are obvious from the first entry – 'The Arab's farewell to his horse' and various cuttings and illustrations, but the book itself she must have kept for many years, as the handwriting becomes much more mature towards the end. Tucked into the pages, though not pasted in, are contributions from other people.

Albums, or autograph albums as they eventually were known, became more and more popular with young people. Gradually their character altered as changing leisure activities and new interests crept in. They progressed from mainly poems and sentimental sayings, to include more complex drawings and paintings interspersed with pages of autographs alone.

In an album dated 1888 nearly all the contributors illustrated their rather sentimental entries, some of them very skilfully.

An adult's album, also dated 1888, consisted entirely of written and skilfully drawn or painted contributions from friends.

Another one dated from 1902–12 starting with childish entries and ending with cheekier ones as fashions both in dress and behaviour started to alter. The third one, dated just a few years later has some more accomplished entries perhaps mirroring the more serious nature of the owner and her friends.

As well as illustrating how society and tastes were altering up to and during the First World War, these and similar albums do more than that. They are a touching reminder of the youth of those you might have known only in extreme old age.

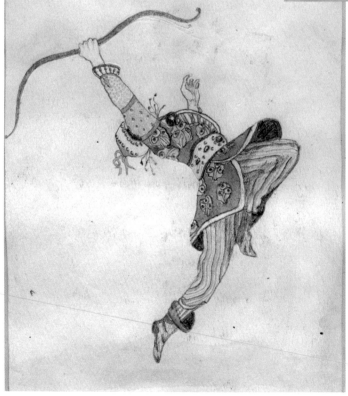

Illustrations from two albums dated from 1909–1915. Their contents reflect perhaps the different tastes of their friends as well as the changing social scene.

Elements from a 1950s scrapbook illustrating packaging from that era. Notice how the early examples of frozen fruit had metal tops.

Sainsbury and Mac Fisheries were leaders in the design of packaging in those days.

CHAPTER 9

Scrapbooks professional or personal

Chronicles can be stretched to include visual records such as professional or personal scrapbooks and sketchbooks, annotated or not. They too are a part of personal records – whether intrinsically or historically valuable or because they reveal more of the person who kept them, and the period in which they were collated. Many professionals keep scrapbooks early in their careers – and often continue throughout their lives. Artists and architects, engineers too, no doubt, sketch parts or whole of scenes, buildings or objects of interest to them at the time. Other professionals keep cuttings of visual reference, and often annotate them.

In my first job as a young designer in a traditional textile studio, my first scrapbook consisted of unusual flowers – drawn, photographed and clipped from seed catalogues. Then came illustrations of Chelsea figurines or something likely to be useful for Chinoiserie, or *toiles de jouy*, toys for nursery prints, etc. Some of these are well preserved in scrapbooks and even after nearly 50 years bring to mind the specific designs which they were used for. Other piles of reference material which I had never got around to mounting I now remember with regret. They became crumpled and torn until eventually several large paper bags full had to be discarded.

A page from a 1950s scrapbook showing some of the many styles of brush lettering used in advertising in the days when commercial artists were skilled in free lettering and few suitable display types were available.

The speed with which such professional scrapbooks can become history was brought home to me quite forcibly a couple of years ago. A small notice, in a copy of *Good Housekeeping*, read 'Wanted; packaging dating before 1980, for a permanent exhibition. Reply to the Science Museum'. Before 1980? Surely there would be plenty around. When I telephoned the curator I was told that this was not so. Back to scrapbooks – my second job had been as a packaging designer in the early days of that industry, at the beginning of the 1950s. I had amassed several scrapbooks of items of packaging that had attracted me for various reasons. There were also illustrations and advertisements which I had kept more for references of lettering or colour combinations than for any concern with their content. In addition, when I finally left the studio, in a rush, to marry and go abroad to live, I had preserved a whole drawer full of loose examples of bread, soap, biscuit and confectionery wrappings. The museum curator was delighted. As she said: 'Attractive biscuit or cocoa

tins are not so difficult to find, but paper wrapping would often be soiled and inevitably thrown away.' A suitable selection was chosen to wrap around products to display in a 1950s larder – and then we turned our attention to the contents of the scrapbooks in more detail. Items that I had kept for purely the 'decorative art' aspect revealed some fascinating forgotten information.

Only thirty years after the advent of frozen food who remembers that frozen fruit or vegetables once came in metal ended cartons? I had kept a range of Mac Fisheries packaging because I admired the design – but it was what it showed about the early technology which was more interesting. Maybe a railway museum ought to be offered the pamphlet on another page, which described the difference between a 1/- and a 1/6 food box on British Rail. I had kept it, probably without even reading it, because of its interesting layout.

There was still something missing, as far as the Science Museum was concerned. The exhibition was due to have a life of 15 years, so it was obviously quite a substantial matter. It had been sponsored by a well-known grocery chain, yet no early packaging designs were available from that particular company. It seems incredible to me that such important firms should not keep archives, particularly as that grocery chain led the way, not only in food technology and marketing, but also in

This fish, found in one scrapbook, came (after considerable pleading from me) from a huge mobile that was suspended from the ceiling of the famous Illum store in Copenhagen in the mid 1950s. The decoration was to celebrate the discovery of the coelacanth that had previously thought to be extinct.

More examples of lettering from scrapbooks that are typical of an age when hand lettering was a very necessary skill.

Be careful what type of adhesive you use in your scrapbook. Some kinds can ruin your material. If in doubt ask for expert advice.

packaging design. Anyhow all was not lost. There were very few of us in that field in the 1950s, and we mostly knew each other. The designer from that particular company happened to be an old friend, and of course he had kept examples of his own work from that decade – so from the depths of his overcrowded drawers, came some unused samples and the gap was plugged. Designers are useful hoarders of ephemera, be it packaging, postage stamps (yes, even stamps have to be designed), or publicity folders, we tend to be careful to keep examples of our early work. You could look at it another way. What we have preserved has become valuable because everyone else has disposed of theirs.

The next set of my scrapbooks charted my

changing of jobs. They are filled with samples of lettering. Before the days of stick on letraset letters and long before the computer made hand drawn lettering unnecessary, all of our work was done that way. Magazine headings were done in attractive brush scripts that would cost a fortune now to commission from anyone skilled enough to produce it. Anyhow it is all there for anyone interested, although a bit discoloured at the edges.

The late Kathleen Strange left her six scrapbooks in my care. They will eventually join my own in the archives of The Victoria and Albert Museum where together they will be valuable in projecting a graphic image of what was happening in the middle of the twentieth century in our areas of expertise. At the same

A few examples from Kathleen Strange's copious scrapbooks that reflect the graphics of the mid 20th century.

Also, her membership card from the International Register of Private Presses.

time they reflect Kathleen's personality and tastes. She had a small private press and her interests ranged over typography in all forms, from history to advertising. Her typographic scrapbooks cause interest whenever they are shown. They do not include the kind of glossy examples that you see in coffee table books but snippets of carefully chosen bits that are unlikely to have survived elsewhere. There are examples and articles that everyone else probably discarded and forgot about long ago, and wonderful illustrations, giving a personal and individual view of the printed word over fifty years.

She was an enthusiastic member of The Society for Italic Handwriting, and her collection

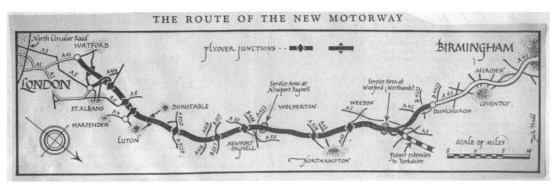

Kathleen Strange kept many interesting letters, particularly from members of The Society for Italic Handwriting. She had an interesting method of mounting them. Pasting down an envelope, she fanned each selection out, making both a decorative display, but more important, preserving any of them from damage.

A few of the many Christmas cards kept by Margaret Gash.

A different area was covered by a young botanist in the 1940s before she started her career in another field altogether. She searched out and collected (or in the case of rare varieties observed and sketched) the wild flowers of her native Kent. Each year she assiduously noted the exact date and habitats of every specimen. Her findings were recorded in officially printed volumes that were eventually lodged in the county library. Now at least there should have been should have been a record of sites and species long lost to housing estates and roads.

Today there is no trace of what has happened to them since they were donated. Unfortunately this does happen from time to time. Maybe they were considered of no importance, or took up too much room and were discarded. Sometimes it is better to keep things in the family, though these obviously were more suitable for a proper archive.

A scrapbook may have no purpose other than pleasure and the joy of reminiscing for the collector. Margaret Gash, a retired art teacher has kept a striking collection of Christmas cards designed by her former pupils. Even this scrapbook might have a general rather than decorative interest in the future. Christmas cards have come a long way from their origins in Victorian days. From religious prints, snow scenes or sentimental depictions of robins, these examples show designs at the start of the 21st century. What will be fashionable in another hundred years?

There comes a time for everyone when it comes impossible to retain everything. On

includes letters from many of those connected with that movement, plus a voluminous collection of handwriting samples from all age groups and in different styles – all carefully labelled and annotated. That alone is remarkable, and of great value to those interested in the subject. These scrapbooks and her accompanying writings deserve a whole book to themselves, not just these few sentences.

As you can tell from other contributions of hers in this book, she was a true example of a keeper of chronicles.

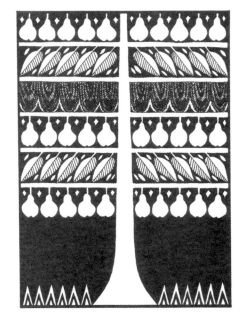

Some sketches of some of my children's favourite toys ended up some time later around a mug, designed by Pat Savage, for The Children's Society charity.

retirement there is often a move to a smaller house, but please remember do not destroy those scrapbooks, examples, archives or whatever you call your store of professional memorabilia. Professional scrapbooks from almost any discipline, would be of interest to the appropriate professional institute. Apart from specialist collections such as the ephemera at Reading University, there are museums all over the country who might be grateful for them – the more unusual the collection the better.

Someone will always be interested in your scrapbook. Seeing your collection through other eyes can be fascinating – and even the exercise of phoning around curators to see who would like to care for your treasures opens up some interesting avenues. That way you forge new contacts and make new friends. Remember, you are offering something of potential interest, you are not asking a favour. There is no need to be defensive about your collection. It is just what someone, somewhere is looking for. If it is not quite right for the first person who you contact, most likely he or she will be able to pass you on to someone who will be interested. There is more about how to find a suitable home for your collection in Chapter 12.

Pat Savage trained as a sculptor but nowadays concentrates on batiks and printmaking. Like so many artists she keeps copious sketchbooks which she either uses as, in this case a preliminary drawing for a finished work, or to store for future reference. Her sketches of preparations for a production of Joseph and his Technicolour Dream Coat, in Cambridge, slowly developed into a finished work.

Most artists keep their sketchbooks as a archive and as a repository of ideas for future use, as well as a record of progress and changing style.

Drawings from Pat Savage's sketchbook and the resulting finished print.

Sketchbooks

The sketchbooks of famous people sometimes merit publication, either during their lifetime or posthumously. One such example, privately printed in 1905, concerns the life and work of Hans Christian Anderson. In this unusual publication separate sheets, are collected in a small folder, entitled (in four languages) *A picture book with pictures*. This seems a strange title considering it comprises excerpts from several of his notebooks which seem to be dedicated to different people. They comprise annotated photographs, but predominantly sketches and examples of his famous paper cutouts.

A drawing, handwriting and one of his paper cutouts from Hans Christian Anderson's folder *A picturebook with pictures*, printed by Winkel & Magnussens Kunstforlag, Copenhagen, 1905.

There is a family connection here as Hans Christian Anderson, in his old age, lived as a guest in the home of one of our Danish relatives.

1. Flower with *sepals*
2. Do on *the pollinia* the Edges
3. 1 pair of *pollen*

A VERY VICTORIAN PASSION

The Orchid Paintings of John Day

PHILLIP CRIBB &
MICHAEL TIBBS

BLACKER PUBLISHING *and*
THE ROYAL BOTANIC GARDENS, KEW

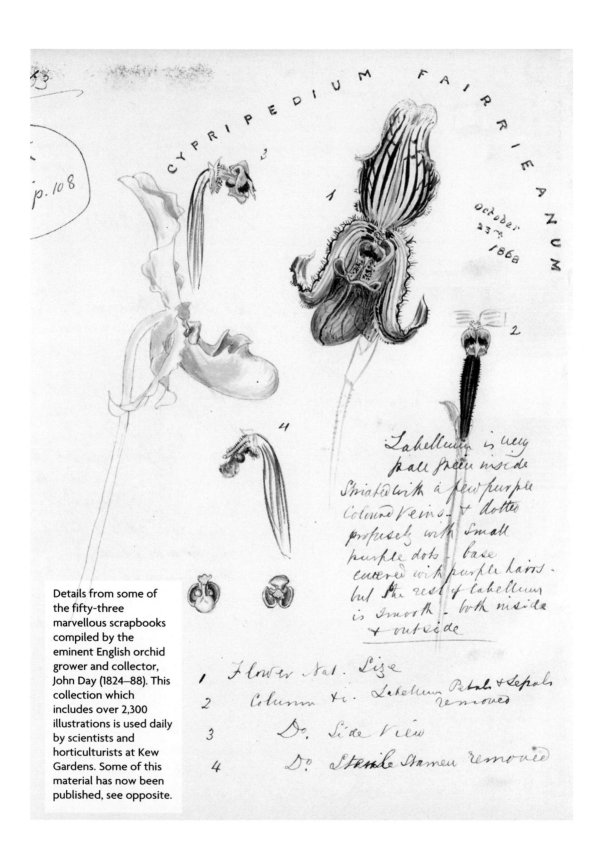

Details from some of the fifty-three marvellous scrapbooks compiled by the eminent English orchid grower and collector, John Day (1824–88). This collection which includes over 2,300 illustrations is used daily by scientists and horticulturists at Kew Gardens. Some of this material has now been published, see opposite.

Pages from the
childhood sketchbook of
Margaret Goodrich.

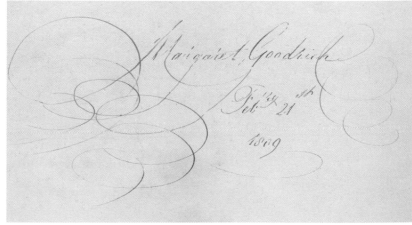

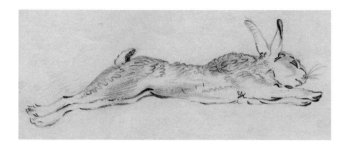

Margaret Goodrich's sketchbook is part of the collection from her family some of which appear elsewhere in this book. There is no indication of how old she was in 1809 but her detailed work illustrates the techniques that were taught in those days.

A mid-nineteenth century sketchbook belonging to Elizabeth Waley shows even more meticulous drawing and shading. It is not known whether these were preliminary sketches for more finished work or not, but she was an accomplished painter who studied with some of the famous artists of the day.

From the sketchbook of Elizabeth Waley.

Simon Waley's sketches
of ships in Boulogne
harbour.

You can tell just as much about a character from the drawn trace as you can from the written. Take these sketches of ships in Boulogne harbour by Simon Waley: they are completely different and much freer and more modern than Elizabeth's. Yet these two were brother and sister. I would have loved to have known Simon, my great-grandfather. He was a man of many talents who died very young. He was also a musician and here is a page from his music notebook. He composed mainly religious music, which is still played at weddings and other family occasions. It is through such memorabilia that we can reach back and get to know our ancestors.

The handwriting, drawing and even music manuscripts, can tell us much about the character of our ancestors. It is not only their skills as artists or musicians that is revealed.

VOL. IV.

LECTURES

on

Mathematics.

Delivered in

UNIVERSITY COLLEGE, LONDON.

by

Professor De Morgan

Session 1861 1862.

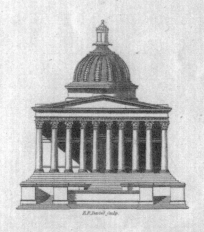

R.F.Daniel sculp.

WALTON & MABERLY, UPPER GOWER STREET.

CHAPTER 10

Schoolbooks, reports etc.

Few people have the space to keep their children's school books or even their reports. They usually get discarded as soon as they are brought home at the end of the year. However, as a resource to those interested in the history of education, the way they record the changes that have occurred, even in the last few decades, make the few that survive invaluable. Those from a century or more ago remind us of the way our ancestors learned in a very different environment. They also reveal much about the individual student or teacher.

Look at the illustration opposite. It is the first page of a notebook filled by a nineteen-year-old university student who was studying mathematics at London University in 1861. It has been handed down in my husband's family for generations and is bound for one of our two grandsons, both studying the subject. The contents are interesting enough to anyone who has reached the level of calculus, but it discloses more than that. The front page of this hard backed book is printed by the university with suitable gaps for the student to fill in dates, subject and lecturer. It suggests that, in the absence of textbooks in those days, the student had to make his own from lecture notes, which had to be precise. The subsequent three hundred pages attest to the meticulous care taken by the student in recording every detail.

This book consists of three hundred pages of notes written during lectures on calculus. It reveals that London University printed such books for students to use presumably where there were as yet few textbooks on certain subjects.

To be of maximum use to researchers in the future, examples should be annotated as extensively as possible (on a separate sheet). If you have a considerable amount of material an archivist from the institution that is to receive them would advise or maybe assist you in this task.

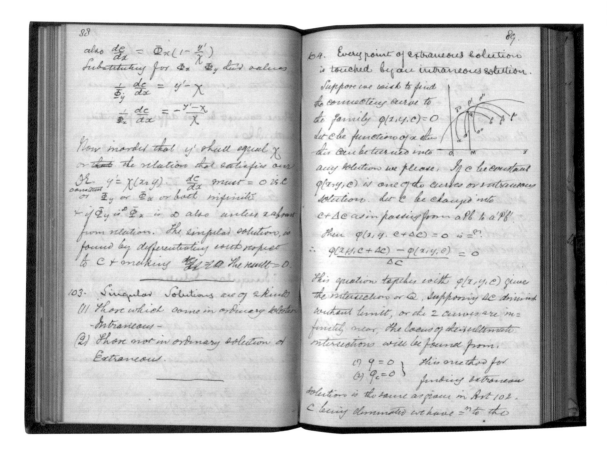

A page of the book, filled with notes on calculus, dated 1862.

On a second visit to Adelaide, in the window of the same shop where several years earlier the diaries were found (see p22), was an interesting handwritten maths teaching book. It must have a strange story to tell – this slim volume, covered in marbled paper – because inside is a stationer's label from Yarmouth, as well as the writer's Ormesby address and the date 1821. How did it end up in South Australia? Anyhow, lucky were the students to have learned from this tutor, wherever they studied. The explanation of every simple rule of mathematics is clearly and

In 1821, in Ormesby in north east England, John Elliot, presumably a teacher, started to write and illustrate his own mathematics book. Apart from his innovative techniques and attractive illustrations, some of which are shown on the next page, this book presents a mystery. How did it turn up in Adelaide, South Australia over a hundred and fifty years later? Did Elliot emigrate or did a tourist buy it in England and later sell it? Parish records or lists of emigrants might provide an answer.

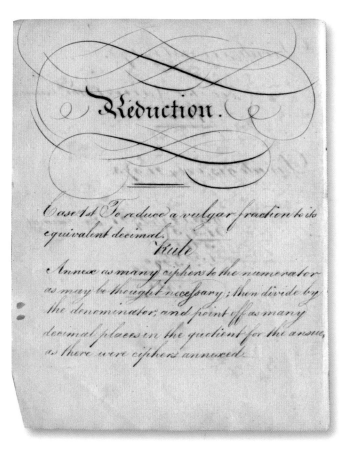

beautifully laid out but the most innovative aspects are his illustrations teaching the rules of geometry.

One of his illustrated examples is described this way:

'To calculate the height of a steeple: Suppose Helmsby steeple is thirty-seven yards distant from the highway and a line ninety yards long will reach from the road to the top of the Steeple, I demand the perpendicular height of it.'

Another went like this: 'A castle wall there was, whose height found it was to be a hundred

Some of John Elliot's illustrations from his 1821 handwritten teaching book.

It would be of particular value for researchers to see a series of books of the same subject, such as these maths books, which range over a considerable period of the nineteenth century.

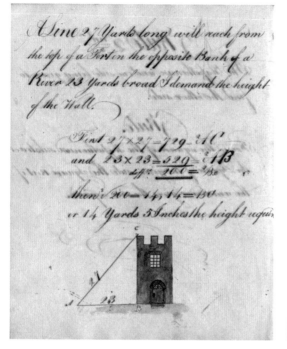

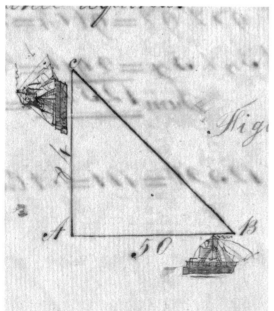

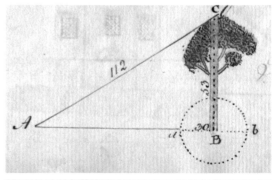

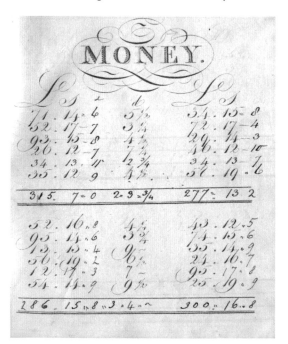

When the nation complains the rulers should listen to their voice.

In the days of youth, the multitude eagerly pursue pleasure as its chief good.

faults 3   3 faults

feet from the top to the ground, Against the wall was a ladder stood upright of the same length as the castle. A waggish youth did the ladder slide. How far the top of the ladder did fall by pulling out the ladder from the wall.'

The name of the church and a castle confirmed that this book came from England.

A small collection of schoolbooks from an extended family provide an overview of education during the nineteenth century, and

More representative of the time are some of Mary Anne White's schoolbooks dating from 1810 onwards. Above: parsing from her 1814 book of grammar exercises. Below left: a maths book printed in 1806 by R Langford, consisting of fifty solid pages of sums, see also next pages.

Below: a page from her handwritten book dated 1815 that she called Sums out of Worthington's Arithmetic.

These and other books from the extended Goodrich family provide a valuable picture of education in the nineteenth century.

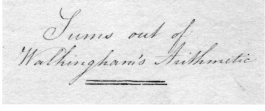

HUGHES'S
COMPLETE ARITHMETICAL TABLES.

Printed for T. & R. HUGHES, 35, Ludgate-street.

Numeration Table.

Units...........	9
Tens...........	98
Hundreds........	987
Thousands.......	9876
Tens of Thousands..	98765
Hundreds of Thous.	987654
Millions.........	9876543
Tens of Millions....	98765432
Hundreds of Millions	987654321
Thousands of Mil.	9876543219
Tens of Thous. Mil.	98765432198
Hund. Thous. Mil.	987654321987
Millions of Millions	9876543219876

A Table of Pence and Shillings.

Pence	s.	d.	Shil.	£.	s.
20 is	1	8	20 is	1	0
30 --	2	6	30 --	1	10
40 --	3	4	40 --	2	0
50 --	4	2	50 --	2	10
60 --	5	0	60 --	3	0
70 --	5	10	70 --	3	10
80 --	6	8	80 --	4	0
90 --	7	6	90 --	4	10
100 --	8	4	100 --	5	0
110 --	9	2	110 --	5	10
120 --	10	0	120 --	6	0

4 Farthings make 1 Penny
12 Pence 1 Shilling
20 Shillings
240 Pence } a Pound.
960 Farthings }

COINS.

	VALUE. £. s. d.	WEIGHTS. oz. dwt. grs.
Five Moidores are..	6 15 0	1 14 15
Half ditto.........	3 7 6	0 17 7½
Three Pounds Twelve	3 12 0	0 18 12
Half ditto.........	1 16 0	0 9 6
A Moidore	1 7 0	0 6 22
Half ditto........	0 13 6	0 3 11
A Guinea	1 1 0	0 5 9
Half ditto	0 10 6	0 2 16½
One third ditto.....	0 7 0	0 1 19
Eighteen Shillings ..	0 18 0	0 4 15
Half ditto	0 9 0	0 2 7½
A Mark...........	0 13 4	0 3 8
An Angel.........	0 10 0	0 2 12
A Noble..........	0 0 8	0 1 16
A Crown..........	0 5 0	
Half ditto	0 2 6	

Note.—Each Grain of Gold is 2d. and each Pennyweight is 4s. at 4l. per Oz.

Even Parts of a Ton.

cwt. qrs.		
10 0	is	Half a Ton.
5 0		1-4th
4 0		1-5th
2 2		1-8th
2 0		1-10th
1 1		1-16th
1 0		1-20th

Even Parts of a Hundred.

qrs. lb.		
2 0	is	Half Cwt.
1 0		1-4th
0 16		1-7th
0 14		1-8th
0 8		1-14th
0 7		1-16th

A Table of Customary Weight of Goods.

	lb.
A Firkin of Butter is........................	56
A Firkin of Soap is.........................	64
A Barrel of Pot Ashes is....................	200
A Barrel of Anchovies is...................	30
A Barrel of Candles is.....................	120
A Barrel of Figs, from 96lb. to 2 Cwt. 3 Qrs.	
A Barrel of Soap is.........................	256
A Barrel of Butter is.......................	224
A Puncheon of Prunes is 10 or 12 Cwt.	
A Fother of Lead is 19 Cwt. 2 Qrs............	2184
A Stone of Iron or Shot is...................	14
A Stone of Butchers' Meat is.................	8
A Gallon of Train Oil is....................	7½
A Faggot of Steel is........................	120
A Quintal of Fish, in Newfoundland, is.......	100
A Stone of Glass is........................	5
A Seam of Glass is 24 Stone, or.............	120
A Ream of Paper is 20 Quires	
A Quire of ditto — 24 Sheets.	

Cloth Measure.

4 Nails 1 Quarter of a Yard
4 Quarters 1 Yard
5 Quarters 1 Ell English
3 Quarters 1 Ell Flemish
6 Quarters 1 Ell French.

Scotch and Irish Linens are bought and sold by the Yard English; but Dutch Linens are bought by the Ell Flemish, and sold by the Ell English.

Wool Weight.

7	Pounds make 1 Clove
2	Cloves —— 1 Stone*
2	Stone —— 1 Todd
6½	Todds —— 1 Wey
2	Weys —— 1 Sack
12	Sacks —— 1 Last.

* A Stone of different Goods, and at different places, varies much.

Cubic Measure.

1728 Cubic Inches make 1 Foot
27 Cubic Feet, 1 Cubic Yard
This comprehends Length, Breadth, and Thickness.

Coal Measure.

4 Peck make 1 Bushel
9 Bushels 1 Vat or Strike
36 Bushels 1 Chaldron
21 Chaldrons 1 Score

HAY.

56lb. old Hay } is 1 Truss.
60lb. new ditto }
36 Trusses is 1 Load.

These pages of comprehensive tables were pasted in to the front of Mary Ann White's maths book, despite simpler tables already in the back of the book. This suggests that the unfortunate students were expected to memorise all this complex information.

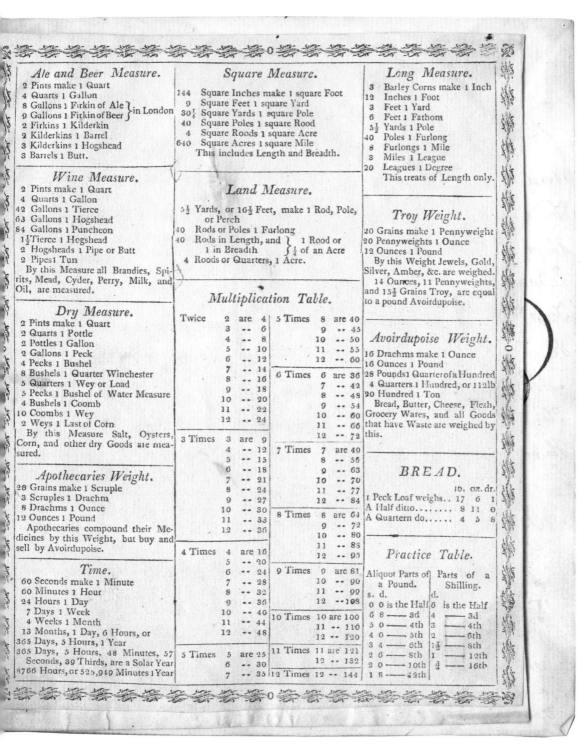

Ale and Beer Measure.

2 Pints make 1 Quart
4 Quarts 1 Gallon
8 Gallons 1 Firkin of Ale } in London
9 Gallons 1 Firkin of Beer
2 Firkins 1 Kilderkin
2 Kilderkins 1 Barrel
3 Kilderkins 1 Hogshead
3 Barrels 1 Butt.

Wine Measure.

2 Pints make 1 Quart
4 Quarts 1 Gallon
42 Gallons 1 Tierce
63 Gallons 1 Hogshead
84 Gallons 1 Puncheon
1½ Tierce 1 Hogshead
2 Hogsheads 1 Pipe or Butt
2 Pipes 1 Tun

By this Measure all Brandies, Spirits, Mead, Cyder, Perry, Milk, and Oil, are measured.

Dry Measure.

2 Pints make 1 Quart
2 Quarts 1 Pottle
2 Pottles 1 Gallon
2 Gallons 1 Peck
4 Pecks 1 Bushel
8 Bushels 1 Quarter Winchester
5 Quarters 1 Wey or Load
5 Pecks 1 Bushel of Water Measure
4 Bushels 1 Coomb
10 Coombs 1 Wey
2 Weys 1 Last of Corn

By this Measure Salt, Oysters, Corn, and other dry Goods are measured.

Apothecaries Weight.

20 Grains make 1 Scruple
3 Scruples 1 Drachm
8 Drachms 1 Ounce
12 Ounces 1 Pound

Apothecaries compound their Medicines by this Weight, but buy and sell by Avoirdupoise.

Time.

60 Seconds make 1 Minute
60 Minutes 1 Hour
24 Hours 1 Day
7 Days 1 Week
4 Weeks 1 Month
13 Months, 1 Day, 6 Hours, or
365 Days, 5 Hours, 1 Year
365 Days, 5 Hours, 48 Minutes, 57 Seconds, 39 Thirds, are a Solar Year
8766 Hours, or 525,949 Minutes 1 Year

Square Measure.

144 Square Inches make 1 square Foot
9 Square Feet 1 square Yard
30¼ Square Yards 1 square Pole
40 Square Poles 1 square Rood
4 Square Roods 1 square Acre
640 Square Acres 1 square Mile
This includes Length and Breadth.

Land Measure.

5½ Yards, or 16½ Feet, make 1 Rod, Pole, or Perch
40 Rods or Poles 1 Furlong
40 Rods in Length, and } 1 Rood or
1 in Breadth } ¼ of an Acre
4 Roods or Quarters, 1 Acre.

Multiplication Table.

Twice	2	are	4	5 Times	8	are	40
	3	--	6		9	--	45
	4	--	8		10	--	50
	5	--	10		11	--	55
	6	--	12		12	--	60
	7	--	14				
	8	--	16	6 Times	6	are	36
	9	--	18		7	--	42
	10	--	20		8	--	48
	11	--	22		9	--	54
	12	--	24		10	--	60
					11	--	66
3 Times	3	are	9		12	--	72
	4	--	12				
	5	--	15	7 Times	7	are	49
	6	--	18		8	--	56
	7	--	21		9	--	63
	8	--	24		10	--	70
	9	--	27		11	--	77
	10	--	30		12	--	84
	11	--	33	8 Times	8	are	64
	12	--	36		9	--	72
					10	--	80
					11	--	88
4 Times	4	are	16		12	--	96
	5	--	20				
	6	--	24	9 Times	9	are	81
	7	--	28		10	--	90
	8	--	32		11	--	99
	9	--	36		12	--	108
	10	--	40	10 Times	10	are	100
	11	--	44		11	--	110
	12	--	48		12	--	120
5 Times	5	are	25	11 Times	11	are	121
	6	--	30		12	--	132
	7	--	35	12 Times	12	--	144

Long Measure.

3 Barley Corns make 1 Inch
12 Inches 1 Foot
3 Feet 1 Yard
6 Feet 1 Fathom
5½ Yards 1 Pole
40 Poles 1 Furlong
8 Furlongs 1 Mile
3 Miles 1 League
20 Leagues 1 Degree
This treats of Length only.

Troy Weight.

20 Grains make 1 Pennyweight
20 Pennyweights 1 Ounce
12 Ounces 1 Pound

By this Weight Jewels, Gold, Silver, Amber, &c. are weighed. 14 Ounces, 11 Pennyweights, and 15½ Grains Troy, are equal to a pound Avoirdupoise.

Avoirdupoise Weight.

16 Drachms make 1 Ounce
16 Ounces 1 Pound
28 Pounds 1 Quarter of a Hundred
4 Quarters 1 Hundred, or 112 lb
20 Hundred 1 Ton

Bread, Butter, Cheese, Flesh, Grocery Wares, and all Goods that have Waste are weighed by this.

BREAD.

	lb.	oz.	dr.
1 Peck Loaf weighs..	17	6	1
A Half ditto........	8	11	0
A Quartern do......	4	5	8

Practice Table.

Aliquot Parts of a Pound.		Parts of a Shilling.	
s. d.		d.	
0 0 is the Half		6 is the Half	
6 8 —— 3d		4 —— 3d	
5 0 —— 4th		3 —— 4th	
4 0 —— 5th		2 —— 6th	
3 4 —— 6th		1½ —— 8th	
2 6 —— 8th		1 —— 12th	
2 0 —— 10th		¼ —— 16th	
1 8 —— 12th			

In addition to what they reveal about education these weights and measures are fascinating in their own right.

A girl's essay book. It is beautifully written but has no creative content.

give a different picture altogether. Starting with maths, a beautifully printed book, dated 1806, they demonstrate that there was not much fun to be had. There were over fifty solid pages of sums to complete and the pupil had given up after ten pages.

The other exercise books do not tell us much about the writers. Most of the handwriting is uniformly perfect Copperplate, reducing in size with age. The subject matter is grindingly disciplined. Whether in English, French, Latin (I cannot vouch for the Greek) it consists of page after page of copies of religious tracts, poetry or worthy essays. It must have been torture for any rebellious pupils. There was nothing creative in evidence. The list of contents in one small book give a flavour of what was contained in over one hundred pages of closely written text.

In the back of another neat little book, dated 1888, is something that might be more interesting to historians. It is a reading list, probably added later, by a younger child, judging by the handwriting, It shows her wide choice of books. Over the page are *Tom Brown's Schooldays*, *Little Lord Fauntleroy*, and *Alice in Wonderland* as well as a whole list of Sir Walter Scot's (sic) novels and several by Dickens.

Not many families would have kept their children's work for so long but what about other memorabilia? School reports can be quite revealing. The most amusing, perhaps, are those of famous people who were written off at school as under-achieving pupils and doomed to failure according to their reports. Kathleen Strange was not one of those. She seemed to have been a

Right: A young girl's reading list, undated but in a book dated 1888.

Below: A Handwriting copy book dated 1944, with sentences that surely should have been replaced many years earlier, and a nineteenth-century American copy book.

diligent pupil according to her report, although not so proficient at singing or needlework.

You can discern quite a lot about social changes even from the sentences that pupils were given to copy in their handwriting books. I have a small collection of those old penny or twopenny copybooks dating back to the mid nineteenth century. They are flimsy so few have survived. It surprised me to find that children an late as 1944 were still laboriously copying pages of sentences more appropriate for their grandparents. Naturally the subjects in copybooks from other countries mirrored their own history. Many of the examples reproduced here have appeared in my book

List of books I have read
"C leare ball"
"norton ball"
"Chantry bause"
"Bolmby bause"
"The Broken vow"
"The Child of Clapperton"
"The Dove in the Eagle's nest"
"Kenilworth"
"Quentin Durward"
"an only Sister"
"Rags and Tatters"
"The Kings namesake"
"not a Bit like Mother"
"mrs: over the Way's Remembrance
"He and the World"
"mary's meadow"
"Brothers of Pity"
"Fatherland"
"a great Emergency"
"The Brownies"

To the early explorers the Dark Continent
To the early explorers the Dark Continent
To the early explorers the Dark Continent
To the early explorers the Dark Continent
To the early explorers the Dark Continent
was an abode of mystery and of savage men.

Washington died 1799.   Washington died 1799.
Washington died 1799   Washington died 1799
Washington died 1799   Washington died 1799

1st in Form

.... Winter .... Term.   Year 1912 — 1913

Name... Kathleen Strange ....   Office..................

No. of Excellents........ 15 ....   Form II D...............

SUBJECTS.	TERM MARKS.			EXAMINATION MARKS. Max. 100.		REMARKS.	Teachers' Initials
	No. of Ex. Set	No. Sent in	Aver. Class	Gained	Class		
Scripture— Old Testament			2	90	II	Very good indeed.	M M.
New Testament							
English Literature	1			72	II	Shews interest	M. A.
Grammar	4	4	α	79	II		M A.
Composition	10	10	α	72	II		N. A.
Reading	12	12	α	80	I	Reads well and with good expression	N A
Recitation	4	4	α	76	II	Good. Be careful of the ends of my words.	M M
Writing	6	6	α	80	I	Good and careful	
Dictation	22	22	α	80	I	Very good indeed.	M. A.
English History			α	65	II	Very interested and attentive	M M
French	4	4	α	91	I*	A very good and attentive pupil indeed	J.C.
Oral	34	34	α+			Excellent work	J.C.
Latin							
Mathematics— Arithmetic	18	18	α	98	I*	Good thoughtful work	M A.
Algebra							
Geometry	7	7	β	92	I*	Works well.	M A
Geography			α+	83	I	Very interested	M A
Physical							
Science— Nature Study	6	6	α	67	II	Shews keen interest.	M. A.
Physics							
Chemistry							
Botany							
Brushwork Hygiene	8	8	α			Tries hard, but needs practice	M. A
Music Singing						Has improved.	M A
Drawing	8	8	β	α		Good.	M A
Needlework or Handwork			α			Improved. Always tries.	M M
Drill			α			So smart	M A.
Games			α			Plays a good game.	M A

First Class Work. α   Second Class. β   Third Class. γ

Attendance { Maximum .120.   Absent .....0.....   Late .....-

General Progress   Avg. term's work.

Conduct   v.g. very helpful.

Signatures for untidiness, etc. ....3............

Order Marks

Next Term Begins... January 22nd 1914......

Signed... Kate Coast. Head Mistress.
Marjorie Merrall Form Mistress.
J.C. Strange Parent or Guardian.

Kathleen Strange's report dated 1913. School reports tell as much
about the contemporary curriculum as they do about the pupil.

Handwriting of the Twentieth Century. This is
another use of educational memorabilia, but be
warned, it took nearly half a lifetime to amass
enough material.

Examples of short-lived educational
experiments, such as the Initial Teaching
Alphabet which was popular in the middle of
the twentieth century are of great interest, and

the iniſhial teeching alfabet

juen 23rd mie nues.
ie went tu the zw and ie sau
an elefant and a tieger and a
lieon and a see lion and then ie
went tu macdonalds and ie had

are difficult to find. It was supposed to make it easier for children to learn to spell, and it was hoped by some people to develop this into a system of what they termed Simplified English.

I have been looking through the few of my own children's schoolbooks that have survived. It is time that they were handed on to them to be shared with their own children. It has reminded me of the real pleasure that such things bring, even if, in this case, they have only personal and not historical relevance (at least not for a few decades yet). Many of us regret that we have none of our own early stories or illustrations but it is more than that. In a few generations computer generated texts may more or less take the place of handwritten stories, poems and pictures. Handwriting is already beginning to be considered an obsolescent skill in some countries. Future generations will then be denied those very personal glimpses of childhood that we take for granted, and so regularly deposit in the wastepaper basket.

An example of a child in her first year at school using the Initial Teaching Alphabet (ITA) as late as the early 1980s.

Below: The pleasure of seeing your own, or your children's, early school books make it worthwhile keeping some of them.

Tell me little woodworm
Tell me little woodworm,
Eating thru the wood.
Surely all that sawdust
Can't do you any good.

Heavens little woodworm
You've eaten all the chairs
So thats why poor old Grandads
Sitting outside on the stairs.

War time Christmas Pudding.

Mix together 1 cupful of flour, 1 cupful of breadcrumbs, half a cupful of suet, half a cupful of mixed dried fruit. and if you like, a teaspoonful of mixed sweet spice. Then add a cupful of grated raw potato, a cupful of grated raw carrot and finally a level teaspoonful of bicarbonate of soda dissolved in two tablespoonfuls of hot wat... mix all together, turn into a well .... bowl. The bowl should not .... full. Boil o...... steam for a ...

CHAPTER 11

Cookery books and household lists

Cookery books of whatever age make fascinating reading, and handwritten ones even more so as they often tell you much about the times and taste of the individual. You would think that they would be treasured and handed down from generation to generation, perhaps inspiring others to add to them in turn, but that is not always so.

I found a handwritten recipe book on a stall in a local market, for the princely sum of fifty pence. Although this fascinating document had a local name and address in it, I have tried, but failed, to trace the writer's family.

From 1939 until the mid-1950s, Joan Airey recorded her favourite recipes and personal notes. Her entries chronicled the rationing and austerity years and the lengths that housewives had to go to stretch the rations. Food Facts from the Ministry of Food are pasted in, encouraging healthy eating and listing the month's value of the notorious points system that I remember so well from my childhood. Cuttings from *Women's Weekly*, Constance Spry and Elizabeth Craig vie with recipes from friends and relatives in their varied scripts. Alone, or combined with similar material, it might well justify publication as it chronicles the culinary habits of a wartime housewife. What a pity that the writer's family thought so little of it that it ended up on a market stall.

Ancient handwritten recipe books, such as those from the collection of the late Esther Aresty, an American friend, are very rare. Her collection included an early 15th century manuscript attributed to Apicius a Roman gourmet of the first Century AD. Aresty, in her book *The Delectable Past* (Simon and Schuster 1964), describes it as the earliest cookbook in the

Some of the contents of a Second World War cookery book, found on a market stall, including a report of the points table for so-called luxury goods. The list altered the value of items each month according to what was available. There do not seem to have been any biscuits that month.

FROM THE POINTS TABLE				
Household Milk (on sale soon)			...	2 pts.
Macaroni	...	...	...	2 pts.
Noodles ...	...	...	...	2 pts.
Spaghetti	...	...	...	2 pts.
Vermicelli	...	...	...	2 pts.
Semolina	...	...	...	2 pts.
Pearl Barley ...	...	...	...	2 pts.
Dried Eggs	...	...	...	8 pts. a pkt.
Syrup ...	...	...	16 pts. for 2 lb.
Treacle	...	...	16. pts. for 2 lb.
S.W.1		FOOD FACTS No. 325		

The first page of an early 15th century manuscript attributed to Apicius. The two recipes are for fine spiced wine and honey refresher.

Below: a facsimile recipe for Mawmenny, a hash of capons, from the *Forme of Cury*, 1390. Both these recipes come from Esther Aresty's collection and appear in her book *The Delectable Past* published by Simon and Shuster in 1964.

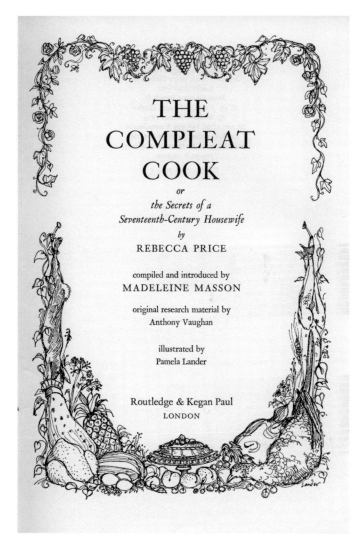

The title page of *The Compleat Cook*. This record of the receipts of Rebecca Price, that she started in 1681 and added to throughout her long life, was compiled and introduced by Madeleine Masson. The book was published by Routledge and Kegan Paul in 1974. Additional research provided biographical details as well as the family tree of Rebecca Price, her will, and an extract from an inventory of the contents of her manor house at Houghton Regis when she died in 1740.

strict sense of recipes: 'Though no proof exists of the date of *De Re Coquinaria*'s first appearance there is no doubt that it was in use until the fifteenth century. My collection includes a handwritten copy made around 1400.'

Her book includes other early recipes where the handwriting adds to the atmosphere of the recipes. She not only chronicled her remarkable collection but interpreted the ancient recipes for modern use, eliminating such esoteric ingredients as the brains of cock sparrows, yet preserving the intentions of the original recipes. She converted handfuls and pecks to modern measures, ignoring the huge quantities that were obviously meant for large households. and tried out all the results on her family – so producing a selection of historic recipes in a modern, usable form for today.

Another fascinating use of a handwritten cookery book, is *The Complete Cook or the Secrets of a Seventeenth Century Housewife* by Rebecca Price (Routledge Kegan Paul 1974). Madeleine Masson, the South African author, and self-confessed collector of ancient cookery books, acquired this a 'vast, calf-bound folio volume', as she describes it, after her son-in-law

This Booke was written by me: Rebecca: Price
in the Yare ⟨1681⟩

At this end of the Booke is all maner of Cookery, and all
sorts of Creams, Custards, sillybubs, posets, jelly, and Caudles,
and all sorts of Cakes, and all maner of Wines, Alle, Beere,
and other drinks, and all sorts of pickles whatsoever:

A page from Rebecca
Price's Receipt Book.

spotted it in an antiquarian bookseller's
catalogue. Her introduction relates how: 'Nearly
three hundred years ago, a young woman living
in Westbury in the county of Buckingham,
compiled a unique document which posterity
would know as *Rebecca Price's Receipt Book*.'

Madeleine Masson was not content with
simply publishing a facsimile, though that in itself
would have been fascinating but probably
somewhat difficult to decipher, nor only a

transcription of the recipes. She and her family
undertook a major research project to trace the
family tree and background of the Prices and
Brandreths. They found the will bequeathing to
her daughter Alice Brandreth: 'My two receipt
Books written by myself one of which said books
being for Surgery and Physic and the other for
Cookery and Preserves both of the said books
being bound with leather and on the inside of
the Lidds of each is mentioned that they were

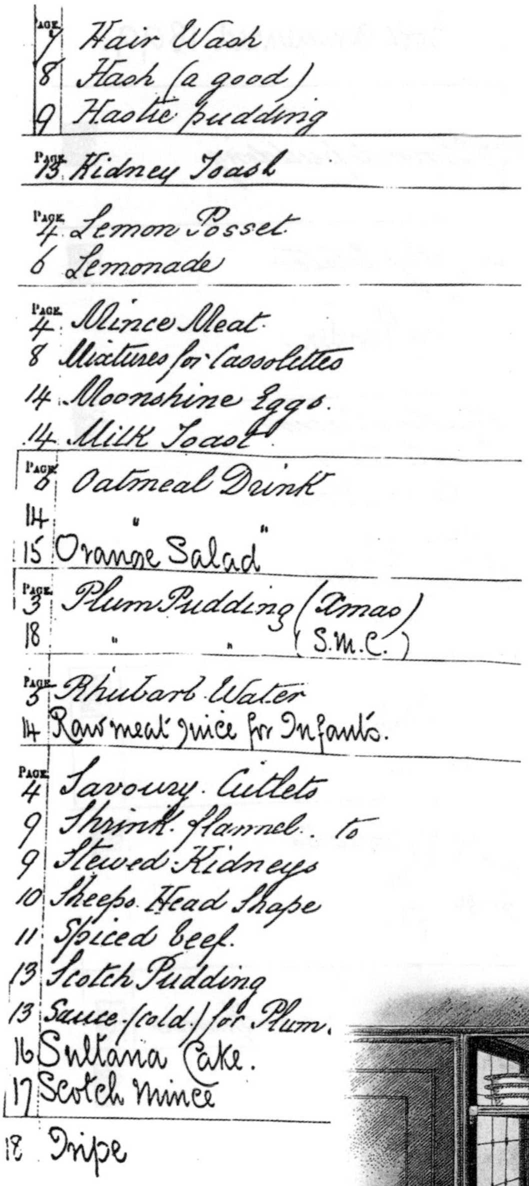
PAGE 7 Hair Wash
8 Hash (a good)
9 Hastie pudding

PAGE 13 Kidney Toast

PAGE 4 Lemon Posset
6 Lemonade

PAGE 4 Mince Meat
8 Mixtures for Cassolettes
14 Moonshine Eggs.
14 Milk Toast

PAGE 8 Oatmeal Drink
14 "
15 Orange Salad "

PAGE 3 Plum Pudding (Xmas)
18 " " (S.M.C.)

PAGE 5 Rhubarb Water
14 Raw meat juice for Infants.

PAGE 4 Savoury. Cutlets
9 Shrink. flannel. to
9 Stewed Kidneys
10 Sheeps. Head Shape
11 Spiced Beef.
13 Scotch Pudding
13 Sauce (cold) for Plum.
16 Sultana Cake.
17 Scotch mince
18 Tripe

Part of the contents from Ethel Boord's recipe book, which she started in 1899.

written in the year 1681 by Rebecca Price (that being my maiden name).'

As a culinary collection this must rate with some of the famous books of cookery published in the seventeenth and eighteenth century. It includes nearly a thousand recipes compiled in 1681 and added to throughout a long life until Rebecca's death in 1740. But much more than that it gives an insight into the life of a city merchant and country squire's family, thanks to the scholarly and meticulous research.

Now, I am not suggesting that many people are likely to be as fortunate as Masson, to find such a treasure even supposing that they could afford it today when such books have leapt in value. Nor are most of us as skilled at researching or bringing matters so vividly to life, but much more modest documents can be of considerable interest to social historians and of course to succeeding generations of the family.

Most people would pass their family cookery books from generation, sometimes adding to them as they do so. Patricia Boord is lucky to have her great-grandmother's, grandmother's and her mother's as well. These she has put

Right: an illustration of a closed range. These 'Patent Kithcheners' began to be made by William Flavel in the 1820s.

In 1890 the Boords moved into Wakehurst Place, near Ardingly in Sussex, built in 1590. Margaret Boord made her mark on the new home by designing a walled formal garden which she called the 'Pleasance Garden'. It appears on her book plate together with her self-awarded title of 'Dame'.

Series of recipe books like these are valuable to social historians as they reflect the changes in households from the days of servants and professional cooks to times of austerity. Even fifty-year-old jottings of recipes from women's magazines should not be disregarded as they reflect the contemporary influences on cooking just as recipes copied from celebrity chef's websites today will be of interest in another half century.

together into a desktop-published book entitled *Boords in the Kitchen* to ensure that all her children and grandchildren should have a copy. An interesting and highly relevant quotation by J A Brillat-Savarin heads the introduction: '*Tell me what you eat and I will tell you who you are.*'

In M Boord's receipt book 1862 recipes are mixed with remedies. So you find Kidgeri subtitled Fish for breakfast, and Mrs Rowe's Mutton as Venison alternating with such useful items as Shooting Boot Grease. A Treatment for Chilblains sounds practical: From mustard made very thick – 1 teaspoon. 1 teaspoon of glycerine and one of olive oil well mixed together, applied night and morning. Plain Pomatum would not be much help today nor a complex instructions on how to wash black silk stockings, but this chronicles how all these were part of the necessities for a good housewife in the nineteenth century. I am not sure that Erasmus Wilson's Embrocation would hardly be approved of today: 'Put the whole of an egg (mixed yellow and white together) into a wine glass. Take same quantity of spirits of turpentine and same quantity of white wine vinegar. Pour all three ingredients into a bottle and shake well and add about two teaspoons of chloroform.'

Ethel Boord wrote: 'I remember an old gentleman with whom my parents were very friendly, Sir Erasmus Wilson, who, I believe was instrumental in bringing Cleopatra's Needle to England'.

Patricia mentions the differing circumstances that influenced the three cookery books. Margaret Boord (1869–1944) certainly had a full

**Party for K's Wedding Anniversary
31st July 1943**

Rabbit Brawn
Peas, Tomatoes, Potato
Salad
Spam

Sweets.
Coffee Rice Cream
Babas au Rhum
Chocolate Mousse
Cream

A menu for a wartime party from Mary (known as Mollie by her family) Boord's 1941 recipe book.

Below: Doctor Andrew Boord 1490–1549 former Carthusian monk and physician, author of *Dyetary of Helth*, written about 1542.

time cook all her life, while Ethel had a cook until World War Two. Her recipe book, an exercise of about 100 pages includes some of her mother's ideas augmented with many of her own. Food rationing was then in force and Patricia describes the selection as: 'Looking to the past for good economical dishes, many from the 18th century when English cooking was at its best.'

A footnote to one of the recipe books tells us that the British pint was 16 oz until 1878, when it was changed to 20oz. So a quart was measured as 32 oz. An 1862 recipe for egg rum said to contain one third of a pint of rum, would not have quite the same strength if anyone copied that recipe today.

The incentive for Mary Boord (1902–1978) to keep a manuscript recipe book was again food rationing. Apart from general recipes, family favourites and newspaper cuttings there are other telling pieces that illuminate the times such as a modest list of *Special foods in store for Xmas*. Then there is a 1943 menu for a party to celebrate a wedding anniversary. The main course was Rabbit Brawn (wild rabbits being unrationed when you could get them), peas, tomatoes, potato salad and Spam.

It is perhaps cheating a bit to mention the first chapter of *Boords in the Kitchen* beacause it concerns the work of an ancestor, Andrew Boord (c.1490–1549), a Carthusian monk and physician, author of *A Dyetary of Helth*. published in 1542. It was of course printed and not hand written. Patricia wrote: 'For Andrew Boorde, diet was the key to health in a way that resonates with the modern reader: "For a good coke is half a physycyon. For the chefe physycke (the counceyll of a physycyon excepte) doth come from the kitchen: wherfor the physycyon and the coke for sycke men muste consult togyther for the preparacion of meate for sycke men"'.

Boorde did not so much provide exact recipes but listed many of the meats, fish, drinks

¶ The .vii. Chapytre sheweth howe the auctor of thys boke, how he had dwelt in Scotland and other Ilandes, did go thorow and rounde about Christendom, and oute of Christendome ; declarynge the properties of al the regions, countreys, and prouynces, the whiche he did trauel thorow.

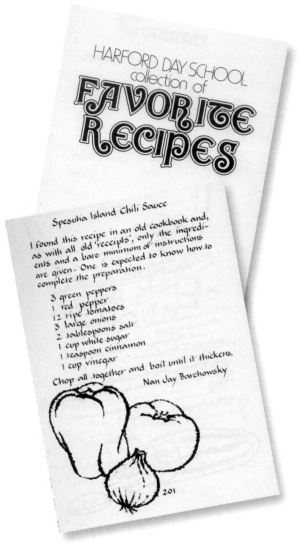

Spesutia Island Chili Sauce

I found this recipe in an old cookbook and, as with all old 'receipts', only the ingredients and a bare minimum of instructions are given. One is expected to know how to complete the preparation.

3 green peppers
1 red pepper
12 ripe tomatoes
3 large onions
2 tablespoons salt
1 cup white sugar
1 teaspoon cinnamon
1 cup vinegar

Chop all together and boil until it thickens.

Nan Jay Barchowsky

201

This book of recipes was a school fund raising project. It is specially interesting because of the multicultural nature of the contributors and the handwriting.

parents of Harford Day School, in 1974. As a fundraising enterprise, they requested copies of favourite family recipes in order to produce a novel cookery book. What is interesting about this collection is the variety of handwriting and the multicultural flavour of the recipes that evidently mirrored the populace. Austrian Pot Roast and Muenster Cheese appeared with Armenian Style Roast and Pork Castilian Style as well as Pork Tenderloin Javanese. Passover Banana Sponge Cake vied with traditional American recipes such as The Ozark Pudding, Pumpkin Walnut Cake, Shad Roe Susquehanna all together with Grandmother's Green Tomato Pie.

This collection harks back to the time when housewives still found time to cook in an imaginative way, trying to keep to cultural or family traditions. I wonder if thirty years on the next generation still carries on the same way.

A rather sad little box came to light in a second-hand repository during a visit to West Virginia. It contained about thirty scraps of paper, torn envelopes, pages torn from account books and diaries, stained, some burned and most written in pencil. Inside the box is written: recipes from, Luray County area 1880–1900. The collection reflects the poverty of the writers, but sadly they are mostly too faint to reproduce. There are some interesting cuttings however. One, an advertisement for an oven thermometer quotes a farmer: 'I don't know how much an oven thermometer helps about baking, but I do know I don't have to cut and carry in more than half as much wood since my wife had one on the oven door.'

vegetable, fruits, and spices that were used in his day and evaluated them in terms of their effects on the human body.

Altogether this work, *Boords in the Kitchen* illustrates how family history, combined with family recipes and a few anecdotes to bring it all to life can make a precious resource for the family and be of interest to the wider reader illustrating how cooking habits altered to keep up with changing times.

Manuscript cookery books tell a lot about the person who wrote them – apart from the actual handwriting. An entirely different use of handwritten recipes was illustrated by the

Some scraps from a box of bits found in West Virginia. Most were too faint to be reproduced, but they pointed to the extreme poverty of the area in the late nineteenth century.

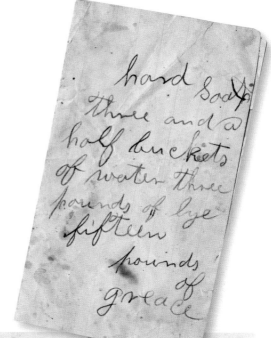

With a

Good Oven Thermometer

on your oven door the same amount of baking can be done with much less fuel.

"Said a N. E. farmer, "I don't know how much an oven thermometer helps about baking, but I do know I don't have to cut and carry in more than half as much wood since my wife has had one on her oven door."

Suggestions for Using the Oven Thermometer

A Good Oven Thermometer Saves Worry and Bad Cooking.

A Poor One is a Source of Annoyance and a Disappointment.

"THE BEST IS THE CHEAPEST."
TIME TABLE.

THERMOMETER DIAL.   TIME IN OVEN.
Beef, Roast, rare.........6.30 o'clock,   8 minutes per pound,

It is not only recipe books but all kinds of domestic lists and records that illuminate the past. Many housewives kept lists of the contents of linen cupboards, dairy books and household accounts among other items that illuminate the past and reveal tantalising details of the different ways our ancestors lived their lives. Garden records abound and are sometimes used to recreate the gardens of centuries past. Game books tell of the results of shoots on large estates or days fishing on the river. Then there are wedding present lists, probate lists and those that value posessions for insurance. These often record the origin and value of items that may have been passed down through the ages and are still in use today. This list is endless.

Detail from John Speed's map of Sussex, 1610

CHAPTER 12

Advice from professionals in the field

Keeping chronicles safe

Notes from a Record Office

Kim Leslie was Education Officer in West Sussex Record Office in Chichester

Right at the beginning of this book Rosemary Sassoon emphasizes that 'Keeping Chronicles' has two quite distinct meanings: it implies not only the recording of information but also its preservation so that it's kept safely for the benefit of future generations.

What follows is some brief guidance garnered from a lifetime's career in archives. Before my recent retirement I spent nearly forty years as Education Officer in West Sussex Record Office in Chichester, representing its work in the local community. I took thousands of people of all ages on tours of the record office, showing them medieval charters for lands around Selsey going back over a thousand years to Saxon times, lavishly decorated Tudor maps, 18th-century deeds for the purchase of slaves in the West Indies owned by a Chichester family, Victorian scrapbooks of colourful advertisements and exquisitely-made greetings cards, even an 18th-century commonplace book kept by a farmer near Petworth with instructions on how to cure a constipated bullock:

For a Bullock that is Sprung say these Words:
Our Blessed Saviour for his Sons Sake Pray

Down the Bladder Blow that he may break.
In the name of the Father and of the Son
and of the Blessed Trinetey Saved may this
Black Bullock be … Then say the Lords
Prayer … three times.

Faith and prayer at work on the farm. And what fascinated visitors just as much as seeing these mouth-watering peeps into the past was the second part of the tour when we looked at the workings of the record office behind the scenes: the processes involved in caring for documents and their storage in air-conditioned strong-rooms.

Showing a copy of a newspaper from the 1930s was the way I always introduced the issue of preservation. Importantly this was not part of the record office collection, but one from home, specially bought for the purpose at a car boot sale. At the edges it was turning yellowy-brown and becoming crisp and brittle. It was suffering because of swings in temperature and humidity, both exacerbated by central heating, although always stored in a cupboard away from the light. Then, to show the damaging effects of daylight, I showed a more recent newspaper from just a month or so ago that had been deliberately left in the conservatory at home, already showing signs of early decay because of the effects of sunshine. Both newspapers used in the demonstration vividly

One of the air-conditioned strong-rooms in West Sussex Record Office showing the movable shelving that increases available storage space. Five million documents and two million photographic images are stored on seven-and-a-half miles of shelving.

made the point about decay (which would ultimately lead to their destruction) because the paper used was cheap newsprint with a high acidic content.

So how does the record office ensure that its valuable collections of parchment and paper documents are well preserved, unlike my two newspapers? Visitors were then shown one of the strong-rooms, its temperature and humidity kept as stable as possible by a huge air-handling plant that takes in air from the outside, then filters and circulates it so that there is constant movement of clean fresh air. If air is still and stagnant with no movement, then mould and mildew can grow on the documents. Temperature and humidity are kept as constant as possible within the range of 16°–19°C and 45–60%. (When quoting humidity, the lower the percentage the dryer the atmosphere, whereas the higher the percentage, the more moisture content there is.) If you want to explore the technicalities behind these measurements then reference can be made to British Standard 5454:2000 laying down ideal storage conditions for documents in a record office. It's accessible on the internet.

We would notice that the strong-room walls have no windows to keep the light out, that the walls are as bare as when they were first built with no paintwork added, so minimizing the chemical content of the atmosphere. The many lights necessary for this huge strong-room go off automatically when not in use to prevent a temperature build-up. On the shelves all boxes are made from high-quality archival board.

By now you are probably thinking that this is all very well for a record office, but how can it relate to your own conditions at home? What can you do yourself, in real practical terms, to guard against damage to all those letters, papers, diaries and albums that have been lovingly and patiently gathered together over the years?

Clearly you will never be able to replicate the same conditions used in a professionally-managed record office. But there are some basic practical steps that can be easily taken to reduce the otherwise damaging effects of heat –

Damaged documents need special treatment for their long-term preservation. Here Simon Hopkins of West Sussex Record Office protects and strengthens an 18th-century paper document by resizing with a weak adhesive to consolidate its surface.

particularly from central heating – and from light and other environmental factors found in the modern home. Always remember that the sooner you start protecting your collection then the longer it will survive for the benefit of future generations. (Your own health and furniture will also benefit!)

Here are some tips to help:

■ Keep stored items away from direct heat such as radiators.

■ Keep stored items away from sunny windows and bright areas. Store in a dark place.

■ Keep boxes off the floor to minimize the risk of any water/flood damage.

■ A cool, dry and stable environment is ideal, but often difficult to achieve at home. One way of reducing the dryness caused by central heating is to use a portable humidifier or, less expensively, radiator humidifiers that work through a small reservoir of water and an evaporating pad to add moisture to a room. In cases of dampness and condensation, use a portable dehumidifier, or again, less expensively, a mini dehumidifier using moisture-absorbing crystals. You can measure humidity by using a hygrometer, sometimes incorporated with a thermometer. All these products can be bought from DIY stores and hardware shops or through the internet. Mould growth and insects such as silverfish will flourish in more humid environments typically found in a centrally-heated house. Be aware of the effects of pockets of stagnant air in little used corners of the house, on walls at the back of cupboards and behind heavy furniture that is rarely moved, especially on outside walls. Mould growth can be minimized by treating with specialist sealers, primers and paints as manufactured by Zinsser, for example. Double glazing, effectively sealing rooms from any draughts and outside air, creates its own problems. Air can be moved around not only by opening windows and keeping cupboard doors ajar, but also by using an electric fan – an oscillating tower fan takes up little space (but don't use in a closed cupboard – you might forget it's on).

■ Avoid storing or hanging anything on external walls if they are damp or prone to more extreme temperature and humidity fluctuations. If framed pictures and documents have to occupy such areas then cut pieces of cork (from empty wine bottles, for example) and stick them on the back four corners so that the frame is separated from the wall.

■ Make sure that anything framed is not mounted and backed with acidic materials. Many framers use acidic hardboard as backing to their frames. The acid leaches out and will attack the document or picture. If this backing is not replaced then an acid-free barrier sheet is necessary to act as a separation between the picture and the backing board. Tell-tale signs of acidic damage to framed prints and documents are spots and stains ranging in colour from brown to reddish-brown to yellowish-brown – otherwise called 'foxing'. Re-mounting and re-backing should be seriously considered if acidic materials have been used. Reputable framers will be able to frame to conservation standards. Always check.

■ Documents, plans and maps should be stored flat, rather than rolled.

■ Make sure that all items are clean, dry and dust free before packing them away. Do not remove dust with a duster which will grind abrasive dust particles into the document. Use a soft brush.

■ Metal fastenings such as pins, paper clips, bulldog clips, tags and staples should be carefully removed to prevent rust and other damage. If a fastening has to be used (is it really necessary?), use brass paper clips, and to ensure that the document is not marked, fold a small piece of paper between the clip and document, using a strip of archival paper or a piece cut from a sheet of high quality writing paper. Staples should not be taken out using a staple remover. Tie bundles together with cotton tape (preferably unbleached) rather than using rubber bands or string which will cut and damage.

- Do not attempt any repairs to a document without expert advice – see below – and never use sticky tape to repair or make a joint. It will discolour, damage the document and eventually lose its adhesion.

- All boxes, folders and sleeves used for storage should be made of acid-free materials. Ordinary envelopes, boxes, folders and plastic sleeves contain chemicals that will cause damage and hasten deterioration. Never store in polythene bags and note that plastic PVC sleeves will damage their contents; one effect is to cause sticking between paper and the sleeve and offsetting of print onto the plastic surface. Instead use archival sleeves that are chemically inert, free of plasticisers and are non-foxing and non-brittling. Transparent sleeves allow you to view without requiring physical handling of the document. A safe protective layer for wrapping documents can be cut from a clean white cotton sheet or pillowslip. Before storing documents in this way make sure that the material is thoroughly washed without the use of any fabric conditioner or perfumed detergent.

- Keep photographs separately from documents and note that many albums readily available on the high street use cheap acidic sleeves and protective sheets that will damage your photographs. Buy only albums made of acid-free materials.

- For scrapbooks – and indeed any other precious books – that cannot be kept in boxes, then storing on well-ventilated shelves is the answer, but beware of dust which is abrasive and may contain airborne pollutants and harbour mould spores. Dust, especially from the top of books, can be removed by a light brush. Be aware that sunlight will damage bindings and cause fading. The use of glass-fronted bookcases should be avoided; they heat up through the glass and limit air circulation. Ideally bookcases should be positioned on the side of the house away from the sun.

Obviously we all want to look after our own priceless collections in the best possible way, but as Simon Hopkins, Senior Conservator at West Sussex Record Office, always emphasizes, we have to be reasonable and realistic about what can be achieved at home. After all, our homes are for living in and for our comfort so we have to strike a sensible balance between professional standards and what is both practical and possible in a home and family environment.

Record office conservators like Simon offer professional advice on the care of documents kept in private custody. You can locate your nearest record office by asking at your local library, or by using the internet. Suppliers of conservation-standard materials plus plenty of advice will also be found on the internet, especially through searching under, for example, 'archival scrapbooking' and 'archival preservation': a vast range of supplies and ideas designed for the amateur collector are listed.

But there is an alternative to keeping documents at home. *Your priceless family documents and papers could be put for safekeeping into a record office and – most importantly – still belong to you.*

Ask the proverbial man in the street where to find out about the past and the response will probably be along the lines of museums and libraries. Most people won't ever mention record offices at all. And yet an astonishing range of information and help can be found in these places.

Record offices are to be found all over the country and are freely open to all members of the public. Each has a vast collection covering the local history of its area. If you want to find out about the history of your house, the history of your family, to find out about your village or town in the past – its schools, the workhouse, the church, the shops – to pore over a 17th-century map, maybe look at some 18th-century prints or Victorian photographs – then the local record office is the place to go. As mentioned already their whereabouts can be checked out at your local library or from the internet.

They started as repositories for looking after the official papers of each local authority. A typical local authority, following a similar pattern throughout the country, is West Sussex County Council. When set up in 1889 it inherited documents going back several centuries with the records of its immediate predecessor, the Court of Quarter Sessions. Quarter Sessions' work covered a wide spectrum of local government as well as criminal matters. Once in business the new county council then started to accumulate records of its own, reflecting its widening spheres of activity – records about education, roads and bridges, allotments, libraries, weights

and measures, children's homes and a great range of other responsibilities.

All these records, both the old (back to 1594) and the new (from 1889) were stored in a muniment room. Year by year the records grew and with them the realization that they needed much better care and organization, this at a time in the 1930s that saw an increasing interest in the nation's local records. And so yet another committee started to meet at County Hall – the Records Committee – and out of their deliberations the County Record Office was eventually established in 1946. It soon started to add documents from sources outside the county council, such as ecclesiastical records – with charters dating from before the Norman Conquest and parish registers of baptisms, marriages and burials of so much value to family historians – and then came the private papers and estate records of major figures in the county landscape such as the Duke of Richmond whose family has lived at Goodwood since the 17th century.

But you don't have to be a major figure with a vast estate to be able to put your own documents in West Sussex Record Office (or in any other office for that matter). Other much smaller collections have come from many hundreds of other people bringing with them maybe a few historic letters from one family, perhaps a single account book from an ancestor's business, a couple of boxes of old family papers or some early house deeds.

Privately-owned documents – whether as a huge collection or just a single item – can be put in a record office in two ways: they can either be

Repairing a 19th-century tithe map with very fine tissue. Adhesives made either from wheat or rice starch are used to avoid damage.

passed over as an outright gift or as a deposit, in the second case meaning they remain the legal property of the depositor (and indeed can always be removed if needed). The advantages in either gifting or depositing are that valuable documents – and I don't necessarily mean valuable in money terms – are kept in safe storage and once sorted and catalogued can be made available for use by other people. They become accessible and usable, not just stuck away in a cupboard or under the bed at home gathering dust. It's important to emphasize that if there are certain documents you wish to remain private and confidential then an embargo on their use can be imposed, stating that they can't be looked at for say ten, twenty or even thirty years. You can stipulate the number of years – they're your papers and it's your choice. Matters of accessibility, copyright and copying can all be discussed with an archivist when considering what to do with your own collection.

What some people do is keep their collection

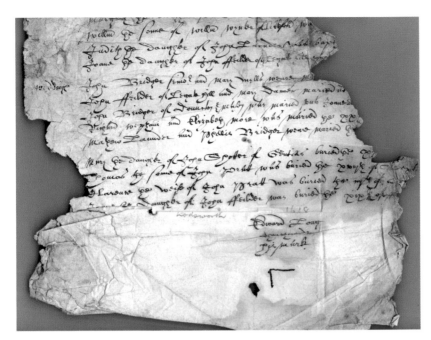

Paper repair: before. This fragile 17th-century document has been weakened by acid attack – note the brown staining – and by poor storage, its edges softened and crumbling away.

at home but stipulate in their will that on their death it is to be given to the local record office; sometimes a deposit may eventually turn into a gift, again a provision that could operate by inclusion in a will.

Problems often arise when a family is faced with a houseful of papers on the death of a relative or friend. A whole house has to be cleared, furniture, clothes, cupboards, the lot – including, in our context here, their personal papers. There's often so much hurry to clear, with little time and inclination to read everything through, then sort it out and decide what to do with it all. And so a sorry story can unfold – with papers either being destroyed, thrown in a skip or sent as waste-paper for recycling. The traces of someone's life gone for ever. The decision to save or destroy rests in your hands.

But you don't have to be faced with this problem. Advice and guidance will be readily given if you make contact with your local record office.

Once a collection comes into a record office

– whether as a gift or a deposit – staff will clean, sort and catalogue. Once catalogued there will be finding aids and indexes to make them accessible. Through these means your documents can be related to other documents and collections held in the record office, giving sense and context within a wider framework of local history.

And one important word of caution: if at all possible a family collection should never be split up.

As an executor I recently cleared the contents of a house belonging to the last survivor of a family known to me for over fifty years. Fortunately the mother, born in 1890, and her two children, had saved virtually everything that had writing or print on it – letters in their envelopes, cards, exam papers, scrapbooks, diaries, household bills, lists, scraps of paper, even some finely decorated paper bags from the Edwardian era with pictures of long-gone shop fronts printed on them.

But sadly a member of the family had started

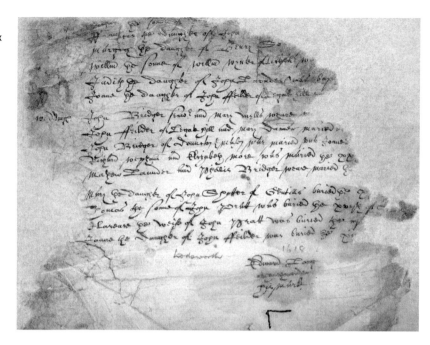

Paper repair: after. The repair in West Sussex Record Office in 1980 involved surface cleaning, washing, de-acidification, resizing and strengthening using wheat-starch paste and Japanese tissue.

to split things up before I knew anything about it. An album of family photographs dating from the 1880s was given to a museum where they decided it would be used in a teaching/handling capacity 'until deterioration'. Think of it, this precious album of family photographs being passed around until it disintegrates! School exercise books were sent back to the mother's school which she had attended from the late 1890s, First World War correspondence had been picked over and a few items sent to a small village museum, some Second World War papers went to a library where correspondence shows they didn't know what to do with them and a Victorian scrapbook went off in another direction. And as soon as I got involved as executor a member of one branch of the family wanted all the papers relating to just their branch sent to them so they could be given to their teenage children – 'the future of our family, in case they might be interested in years to come', the mother said. 'In no way' was my reply, 'they'll understand their own past far better if all the

branches of the family represented by this collection are kept together, and I can guarantee', I went on, 'that they will be professionally preserved for the benefit of the wider family, and others, not just for your children'.

So whilst some of the family papers are sadly scattered, it's encouraging to know that much has been kept together in a record office for safekeeping. The family came from a seaside Hampshire town, but it was still important to keep all the material together even where documents and scrapbooks related to in and around Peterborough and Nottingham, and to time spent in Australia over a hundred years ago. Within weeks of the collection going into the record office, some letters about the blitz over Portsmouth in 1940–1 were being used by an A-level history student and letters are being used for research into the First World War.

So from out of a loft, a wardrobe and old suitcases the papers of just one ordinary family from a little terrace house in Southsea are now safely in Portsmouth City Records Office, stored under proper archival conditions and, importantly, being used by researchers.

I've done exactly the same with my own family papers. My mother's father, born in 1873, never threw anything away, his house and its contents so big it took nearly a year to clear. There are diaries – in the 1890s he recorded every mile he rode on his bicycle, every farthing spent – letters, accounts, photographs, maps, drawings and scrapbooks. As chairman of the Church of England Children's Society, there is correspondence about his work nationally and in running two of its Sussex homes in his village of Rustington. Dr Carruthers Corfield first came down to Sussex nearly a hundred years ago, but his roots are enmeshed deep in the history of Shropshire, at a settlement by the banks of the river Corve near Ludlow (the origin of the Corfield surname in medieval times). His wife's family came from Limehouse, London, one branch going off to Australia. Thus through my grandmother's papers there is information about cholera in London as well as the gold-rush town of Bendigo in Australia because one of her ancestors was a doctor of medicine, first in Limehouse on the Thames, and then in southern Australia. In the early 1850s the doctor took passage to Sydney, landed up in Bendigo, north of Melbourne, and set up a hospital and waterworks company for the gold miners living under the same sort of appalling conditions he'd left behind in London. His son turned his back on the gold rush, exploring the bush with camels, horses, a 'kangaroo dog' and aborigines in search of the remains of the lost German explorer,

Dr Leichhardt, walking all the way to the far north, to the Gulf of Carpentaria and back, an incredible journey of such horrors that led to his premature death aged 37. His grave records him as 'late explorer'. The Corfield Papers thus range near and far, but despite their wide geographical spread their essential unity is given through my grandfather. And so the collection is kept together as one in West Sussex Record Office.

So maybe if you have your own family archive or are perhaps a collector of historical documents or ephemera, you might like to ask yourself if the services of a record office could be as useful to you as West Sussex has been to me.

* * *

Would you like professional advice on the preservation of your collection?

Are you looking after the collection properly under the right conditions?

Do you want to ensure its long-term preservation?

If the answer to any of these questions is 'yes' then I do hope you will make contact with your local record office and see what it has to offer.

From a museum's point of view

Carlo Dumontet is Special Collections
Bibliographer, Word & Image Department,
Victoria & Albert Museum

There is a wealth of information on the Internet
about conservation and preservation issues and
materials.

I have selected three sites which provide
excellent general information:

- Northeast Document Conservation Centre
  (USA)
  www.nedcc.org
- ICON – The Institute of Conservation (GB)
  www.icon.org.uk
- Preservation Advisory Centre (National
  Preservation Office) (GB)
  www.bl.uk/npo

and two sites for suppliers of conservation
material:

- Preservation Equipment Limited (USA)
  www.preservationequipment.com
- Conservation by Design (GB)
  www.conservation-by-design.co.uk

Institutions, especially in times of shrinking
budgets, are always willing to accept meaningful
gifts, but this does not mean that this will always
be the case. Lack of space to store the material
and lack of staff to organize and catalogue it,
may tilt the scale towards refusal.

I would therefore like to give a few practical
suggestions in order to increase the chances of
the gift to be accepted. It is just like selling a
house: you want to show it in its best light to
possible purchasers.

It is important that the archive should be well
organized and sorted by category,
chronologically or any other meaningful way. At
this point a catalogue/check-list should be
produced. If a catalogue is too complex or time-
consuming, a simple and neat word-processed
list might suffice. This will help the institution to
see if the material on offer is worth having. This
list will also help the curators at a later date
when the actual cataloguing of the material will
be carried out. Cataloguing is a time-consuming
operation and any help in this respect will always
be appreciated.

Together with the catalogue/list a few digital
images of the collection should also be provided.
This will give the curators an idea of the size of the
collection and help them in finding space for it.

The more information the curator is provided
with at this stage, the quicker his reply to the
offer will be – an important consideration to
keep in mind.

The sheer size of the collection is not
necessarily of paramount importance. What
matters is that the less bulky and messy it looks,
the better. Many well organized boxes look
friendly, a few disorganized boxes full of bits and
pieces will scare any well-meaning curator. Do
not give the idea that your collection will
present a conservation nightmare.

It is not necessary to store the archive in
conservation material. Good, standard stationery
is perfectly acceptable. This will allow the
institution to accept the archive without the
worry of having to conserve it immediately: it
will give the institution some breathing space.

Printed ephemera

A well organized and kept archive will also allow the institution to put it in temporary storage without fears of fast deterioration of the material.

Remove staples, paper clips, etc. (anything that will rust). Folders bought at big stores with plastic envelopes will be acceptable in the interim for most organizations, even non acid-free boxes (but not shoe boxes). Plastic enclosures are safe for documents only if they are not made of PVC, which will release damaging acids over time. Very big items (wallpaper samples; large graphics) should be kept rolled up rather than folded.

Martin Andrews is Deputy Director of the Centre for Ephemera Studies in the Department of Typography & Graphic Communication, at the University of Reading.

For many people the collection, preservation and study of printed ephemera raises many issues and queries. One of the most frequently asked questions is precisely what do we mean by the term? There have been many debates about a definition of printed ephemera but there is much to be gained from a wide embracing approach, accepting fuzzy edges. Broadly the derivation of the word lies in the Greek epi (about or around) and hemera (a day). The word is also used as the specialist term for the freshwater insect, the mayfly (*Ephemera danica*) that, in its adult winged form, is commonly believed to live for only one day. For astronomers, astrologers and navigators the word ephemeris is used for a calendar or table of days. Even Dr John Johnson, appointed printer to the University of Oxford in 1925 and founder of the extensive and celebrated collection of ephemera that is now housed in the Bodleian Library in Oxford, found it difficult to be precise. He said his collection consisted of '…common printed things … what is commonly thrown away – all the printed paraphernalia of our day-to-day lives, in size from the largest broadside to the humble calling card … from magnificent invitations to coronations of kings to the humblest of street literature sold for a penny or less'. On another occasion he defined it as '…everything which would normally go into the wastepaper basket after use, everything

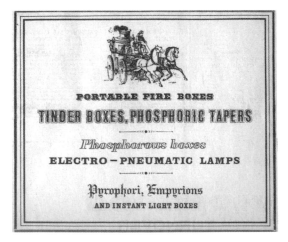

PORTABLE FIRE BOXES
TINDER BOXES, PHOSPHORIC TAPERS

Phosphorous boxes
ELECTRO – PNEUMATIC LAMPS

Pyrophori, Empyrions
AND INSTANT LIGHT BOXES

printed which is not actually a book'. But Johnson's definitions were not meant to be deprecating, on the contrary he greatly valued ephemera as documentation of his world of printing and publishing: 'I keep every trade card of every traveller who comes within the gates [at OUP], and treasure them in my archives. They are among the many gauges of our craft'.

What objects are we talking about when we refer to ephemera? The range is almost as wide as the range of human activity. The structuring and organisation of society, commerce, marketing and advertising, packaging, sport and entertainment, politics and propaganda, education, information and communication, are all examples of activity that generate ephemera. Individually, items of ephemera might seem trivial and peripheral, but cumulatively they can throw a very particular light on history, offering not only factual detail but also an atmospheric and evocative direct link with the past.

There are other areas of confusion and debate. One is the problem of distinguishing when a pamphlet, brochure, and other such minor publications can be described as a book and therefore no longer ephemera. Librarians commonly define a book as being a bound work of thirty-two pages or more. Is a newspaper or magazine to be classed as ephemera? Such publications are given bibliographical status and are kept in libraries and yet are also thrown away after use. This clearly is an issue when looking at journals and popular magazines and documents such as maps. Another problem is how to categorise letters and manuscripts. However, precise and rigid definitions are unhelpful. The circumstances under which the item was purchased or produced and how it was used will be part of how it is categorised. What is important is how this huge and diverse area of material can inform the study of history.

Another common question is 'what use is it and what can we do with it?' Today there is wide recognition of ephemera as an important historical source. Lord Asa Briggs considers 'ephemera' a key word for historians: 'In the reconstruction of the past everything is grist to the historian's mill, and what was thrown away is at least as useful as what was deliberately preserved. As our sense of past times changes, we try to strip away the intervening layers and discover the immediate witnesses.'

Ephemera provides us with a very particular kind of evidence. It offers an opportunity for scholarly analysis as well as a more subjective quality, an almost emotional and tactile response to worn and fingered material, directly handled by the people whose concerns and activities we are trying to understand, material that against the odds has survived and come down to us, often in a fragile state. In an unpublished essay, the ephemerist Maurice Rickards wrote:

An implicit component of every item of ephemera is the reader over the shoulder – the eyes for which the item first appeared; the living glance that scanned the paper even as we ourselves now scan it … Not only can you 'hear their voices' as Trevelyan put it, you can merge your glance with theirs …. You become, as you read, an intimate part of the detail of their experience – not just overhearing them, but momentarily within them....

... As we survey a battered public notice or a dog-eared printed paper, we are aware not only of the sum total of duration (implicit in its wear and tear), not only the buffetings and bruisings that its condition proclaims, but the countless scannings it has undergone – the multitude of readings and re-readings. It is, as you might say, 'eye-worn....'

On another occasion Rickards wrote that ephemera '...has much more than passing validity. Above and beyond its immediate purpose, it expresses a fragment of social history, a reflection of the spirit of its time.... which is not expected to survive, but which can prove to be very useful in research. ...Ephemera, represents the other half of history: the half without guile. When people put up monuments, published official war histories they had a constant eye on their audience and their history would adjust to suit, whereas ephemera was never expected to survive ... so it contains all sorts of human qualities which would otherwise be edited out'.

With the proliferation of junk mail today, many people ask if printed ephemera is confined to more recent times. With the growth of

matcg motabilem quam,pdurerant aque in fpecies fuas· et omne vo
genus fuum. Et vidit deus gp effet tonum:benedixitcg eis dices· Cre
mult...... .... a replete aquas maris:auefcg multiplicentur fup terra
......et mane dies quintus. ....roducat t
an..... .... genere fuo:iuméta ....m fpe
fua..... .....cg eft ita. Et fecit de'tr ....as. ium
et omne reptile terre in genere fuo. .....cg..... ...um: et a
actamus tominé ad imaginem et fimilitudinem noftram:et pfit pifcibu
iaris et volatilibus celi z beftijs.vniuerfecg terre:omnicg reptili quod 1

Shaw's Scripture Cakes

literacy, communications, advertising, and marketing there was a great proliferation of jobbing printing in the nineteenth century, but ephemera existed since the very beginning of printing from movable type. The first dated specimen of Western printing was not a book but a piece of ephemera – an indulgence probably printed by Johann Gutenberg or by his partners Fust and Schoffer in 1454. Although rare, examples of ephemera from the earliest days of book printing have survived. Two copies of a short advertisement printed by William Caxton in about 1478 for his *Commemorations of Sarum Use* still exist. The advertisement promises that the book is competitively priced ('good chepe'). Many figures in past centuries have recognised the importance of collecting ephemera. The seventeenth-century diarist Samuel Pepys had a particular passion for ballads, chapbooks, and other street literature, preserved in the Pepys Library at Magdalene College Cambridge. Amongst thousands of items that form 'a throwaway conspectus of the life and times of a

remarkable Londoner' are 40 or so tradecards gathered from the businesses in walking distance from his home

In our own times, in ironic contrast to the promise of the 'paperless society', our everyday lives are littered with a seemingly ever-increasing amount of ephemeral paper documents that permeate every aspect of our daily existence. 'Junk mail', mostly unwelcome and unsolicited, tempts us to more credit or endless fast food. The vast amount of glossy promotional material, tedious bureaucratic forms demanding our attention, the over-packaging of products and streets strewn with drifts of litter, are a bane of modern life. Yet, in their turn, these documents will reflect our age for the future. From the 'transient minor documents of everyday life' we can have a direct contact with the past through artefacts that were once central to the functioning of society – the etiquette, protocol, private and business life of past centuries and societies around the world.

As has been shown, the world of trade and

REQUIRES ONLY
PALM PRESSURE
TO MAKE A SEAL

POROSAN
Fruit Preserving
CAPS AND
RINGS

commerce can be documented through printed ephemera. It can also reflect other aspects of life: the bureaucratic manipulation and control of society through rules, regulations, forms, records, certificates and permissions that maintain the social order. It reflects the tastes and interests of a period: fashions, hobbies, entertainments, community and social events, sport, travel and the worlds of art and culture. The development of education and communication and the opening up of communities and social mobility can be traced through ephemera. Most events in life are themselves ephemeral. Often the only record of great theatrical and dance performances, musical concerts and art exhibitions, for example, are the programmes, catalogues, posters, tickets and flyers that have survived – particularly for experimental or fringe events.

Ephemera can provide first-hand evidence of

the history of my own subject of printing. Printers' advertisements and letterheads naturally boast of new processes and equipment: the introduction of lithography, photography, stereotyping, electrotyping, process engraving, monotype and linotype can be dated by noting the appearance of such terms. The Koenig steam-powered press was introduced in 1814 but steam power was not in general use by printers until the middle of the century, and its gradual adoption can be traced through letterheads and advertisements. Invoices, bills, and receipts can provide details of costings and profit margins. The other trades and industries associated with book production, such as paper manufacturers and binders, also printed ephemera of a similar nature.

People ask 'if so much material is being generated, how can we possibly keep it all?' Indeed, the mountains of waste in our world show just how impossible this would be. Indiscriminate hoarding of ephemera is to be avoided. If ephemera is to have real value (financial value is another issue), the answer is to focus on a particular aspect of ephemera and create collections that are well documented with thorough research giving the context of the material. Criteria for selecting an approach might include material covering a particular genre of ephemera, historical period, geographical location and source, particular event or product or production technology. The aim should be to create a coherent collection that shows development, diversity, allows comparison and provides a comprehensive overview.

Finally how best to care for and store

ephemera is a common concern. Depending on age, printed ephemera is vulnerable and fragile almost by definition. Often objects have been roughly and frequently handled and made from poor quality materials. Support and protection will be needed to keep items isolated from harmful products and make them safe to handle in the future. Many paper and cardboard products contain harmful chemicals, particularly acids, which will eventually cause damage so mounting materials and storage boxes should be of archival standard and acid free. Paper items are best kept in clear polyester sleeves that are inert and thick enough to provide support. Do not paste items into albums as often the reverse of an item is important – if you mount material then use small hinges to secure the item and again avoid adhesives that contain destructive chemicals and cannot be reversed (gummed adhesive paper tape is best as most self-adhesive materials cause problems). Large objects such as posters have often been folded and these should be carefully unfolded and stored flat. Apart from gentle superficial cleaning, it is best to seek advice about major cleaning and repair.

If the ephemera of the past is a complex subject, then what of the future and the preservation of electronic documents and communications – perhaps we will need a new definition of the word.

How to decipher old handwriting

Peter Foden is a palaeographer and archivist. His contribution will help those faced with the difficulties of reading old documents.

Here are some general points to help you decipher ancient documents;

Documents vary so much therefore it helps to start by getting an idea of the general contents and accustom yourself to some of the vocabulary being used. You can probably decipher some of the simpler words and as you get more into the handwriting the more difficult phrase will gradually become clearer.

The next step is to try replicating the written forms. If they are a recognised style you may be able to find a sample alphabet that will help you. The separate letters are relatively easy to recognise. It is when they are joined and become personalised that your task may be more difficult. So, try to join the letters yourself and words will soon become clearer.

Start by copying down the words as you work them out without trying to make sense of the meaning. Then the next stage is to read through and interpret the document.

You might think that the older the document is the more difficult it will be to read. this is not always the case. Some nineteenth century handwriting may be more illegible than older more intricate but more carefully written ones.

There may be some unfamiliar words or phrases in your document. Do not be put off. There are standard dictionaries, specialised

My dear Philip

Thanks for your two letters, which ought to have been answered ere now but for my lazyness, the climate and the flies

I think you were perfectly right in refusing to commence an arbitrage b...

you have now...

business, and th...

without having...

an arbitrage bus...

Some 19th-century scripts are very difficult to decipher. These are all actual size.

dictionaries such as those concerned with legal terms, and even those concerned with local dialects, to help you.

The reason why, some of the most difficult letters and documents to decipher are the relatively recent ones is because more of the population could and did learn to write after the education acts of the mid-nineteenth century. It became easier to write as steel nibs and proper ink took the place of quills and home made concoctions. Not everyone could write well, unlike the carefully tutored few, and professional scribes of previous centuries. Personal letters and much more material written by ordinary people tends to survive until today in family archives. Meanwhile professional writers, lawyers clerks and court officials for instance, still used conventional specialist styles of handwriting, which might be unfamiliar but tended to be consistent and carefully scribed. Once you get used to the style these documents are relatively easy to read. As for mediaeval and early hands there are both books and online manuals to help you learn about them.

Copperplate, and the slightly simpler Civil Service models adopted during the nineteenth century were devised for speed and regularity and to suit the pointed nibs in use in those days. This meant that every letter had to join to the next. If writers stopped mid-word they risked an ugly blot. The consistent slope and alternating thick and thin strokes led to a strange habit, perhaps meant to be economical but in reality making letters even more difficult to read. Having filled one page, writers might turn the paper through ninety degrees and continue write over the earlier lines. The resulting pattern could be read - but with great difficulty today.

There are several letters that may confuse the modern reader. The small (lower case) open b and p are unfamilar and often deteriorate with careless writing. Several forms of the letter f and s can confuse, even the r and the cursive z for those whose countries have long changed to another form. The capital letters are even more problematic for those writers who have long become accustomed to simple Roman letters. Mixing up I T J, O Q and several others may lead to fruitless searches for your ancestors. It is always worth checking names like Timpson and Simpson or other combinations where you are not sure of the first letter of a name. This is where having a model alphabet and trying out the different forms yourself comes in useful. You also need to recognise the abbreviations of names that were used in documents and even in signatures. Most of them are fairly obvious such as Thos for Thomas, Wm for William, Jas for James, but Jno (John *not Jonathan*) often trips up the novice.

As you get used to working with nineteenth century handwriting you may be able to guess the date of documents and the age of the writer by their handwriting, even though the models were similar. Earlier scripts tend to be more angular and consistent in their slope, while later writers tend to have more rounded writing and open loops, influenced by the different Civil Service models. Slowly, both the letters and slope became more personalised.

Towards the end of the century some more educated or artistic writers adopted quite different models influenced by a revival of interest in classical or renaissance manuscripts, With luck, you might find some parish registers written in these much easier to read hands. Eventually these styles evolved into the italic writing familiar to many today and popular with artists and many others.

While on the subject of models it is worth considering that many countries have had distinctly different models in the past couple of centuries, and still have today. While it may be reasonable to expect to decipher a standard hand, it becomes more and more difficult when writers speed up or personalise their handwriting.

It would be a short hop from collecting and arranging your family papers to researching your family history behind and beyond your collection. While researching you may well have to consult legal documents such as wills, deeds and indentures of all kinds, even manorial court rolls. Such documents were written by professional legal clerks and it was a skilled task. Writing carefully on parchment (well into the last century), they used different styles of handwriting for different purposes, many of them being more rounded than the prevailing hands. They could begin with highly decorated capital letters, and include some words in gothic black letter, or exaggerated Copperplate, for emphasis.

Once again there are certain unfamiliar forms of letters that may confuse today's reader today. Capital letters are often highly decorated and can appear very strange to modern readers. Such letterforms derive from some of the hands in use in the later middle ages and early modern periods:

Large and small legal hands, sometimes called "pigs' bones": characterized by bold vertical lines with angular spidery links. As you might guess, these were used by lawyers, often before 1733 for latin documents, but equally for English letters, petitions, and signatures.

The same writer might be proficient in more than one "hand", switching between them in the flow of a document for emphasis – just as we might change font, embolden or italicize in a word-processed document - or on change of language. Thus Italic was the elegant, modern and therefore legible hand employed for Latin quotations in the sixteenth and seventeenth centuries. But it was also the preferred style for academics, whether writing in Latin or English, and for women including Queen Elizabeth.

Women were never taught "Secretary Hand"; the now very arcane handwriting of professional male scribes during the later 16th and early 17th centuries. Secretary is the acme of English hands. Its texture is regular but not boringly slanted in one direction; some letters are consistently upright, while others fire off at 45% to left or right. Characteristic letterforms include "h" with a huge looped descender, an angular "c" like a little tiny shelf-bracket, and the "backwards" double-looped "e". The scope for confusing twenty-first century readers is myriad. For help I would recommend both the online tutorials on the National Archives website and the book *Palaeography for family and local historians*

Nature requires cultivation to enjoy happiness.

Oppression is most commonly of short duration.

Poverty is commonly occasioned by misconduct.

1450-1750 by palaeographer and researcher Hilary Marshall (Phillimore, 2004).

Gradually the more obscure letterforms were dropped as Secretary and Italic merged into the early transitional forms of Round Hand in the mid to late seventeenth century. Very readable to the modern eye and with varying loops or flourishes on ascenders. Capitals sometimes become quite baroque, but generally these hands are marked by restraint.

Towards the end of the 18th century the "copperplate" ideal, written with finely cut nibs, produced writing whose difficulty lies not in obscure letterforms but in tedious repetition of parallel slanted lines, the upstrokes so fine as to vanish entirely. Written at speed, legibility becomes more and more difficult. It was in reaction to such tedium that innovation in the teaching of handwriting began in the mid-19th century, snowballing with mass elementary education into the unprecedented diversity of hands used in England ever since. If you would like to understand these better, then the expert to read is of course the author of this book Rosemary Sassoon herself: *Handwriting of the Twentieth Century* (Routledge, 1999) includes many examples of alphabets from contemporary copybooks, and concisely charts earlier developments as well as rivalries between teaching methods throughout the last century and longer.

If all else fails and you cannot decipher a certain important document, then look for an "expert" to help you. Most archivists should be able to tackle any English handwriting of the past 400 years, although fewer and fewer can now read the Latin documents that abound from before 1733. Freelance researchers like myself who advertise their palaeographical skills for hire will happily accept such a challenge.

Here is a summary of points to help you decipher ancient documents;

- Familiarize yourself with the relevant technical vocabulary, the phrases and shaping of the piece of writing you are studying

- "Learn by doing": don't just stare at the characters, find out how they were written by trying to form them yourself. Then have a go at joining them into words; what shapes remain when written at speed?

- Transcribe exactly what you see; don't attempt to understand it yet. Leave blanks where necessary.

- Now you can "read" the text, attempting to fill those blanks. Guesswork comes last, not first.

Modern technology as an aid to medieval palaeography.

Margaret Woods specialises in researching and translating medieval documents.

There is for me something magical in being allowed to hold and read an original medieval manuscript; the experience can, for a moment, bring to life the real people involved in a document's creation or depicted in its text. I'm fascinated to know simple facts such as William Tinctor (the Dyer) in 1276 being fined the substantial amount of 12d (old pennies) for making 'an unlawful footpath across the lord's Tyefield'; he had probably been taking a regular shortcut to his place of work – the ground on the edge of the Tyefield where several dyers rented land. Also in the same court record I wonder what on earth lay behind brewsters Lucy Wytemaden, Saburger wife of John Sekestayn and Matilda wife of John Scot refusing to sell ale to certain men of the town.

The medieval documents which reveal such wonderful historical facts are, however, not always held in archives conveniently located for those seeking to research or translate them. The archive in which the 13th, 14th and 15th century court rolls and accounts etc for my town are lodged is 3 hours drive away. Fortunately modern technology can help overcome the obvious constraints of distance and time and enable researchers and translators to work in their own home at their own convenience.

Two of the most straightforward, popular and relatively cheap tools for reprography are photocopiers and micro-fiche/film printers. For many manuscripts, however, these methods are not suitable or permitted e.g. rolls especially when bundles have historically been tied together; also documents of extreme fragility. For such as these digital photography is now widely used; my local archive allows unlimited photographing of documents for £5. The images are transferred from camera to computer and printed; in my experience the outcome is legible and satisfactory.

Other archives permit digital photography only by their own archival reprographer; this is very much more costly. This process is the one I have to use to have convenient home access to the large number of medieval manorial manuscripts relating to my town. The images are sent to me on a CD; this I take to a local printer who enlarges the images and does the actual printing. The combined skills of the professional photographer and printer give an impressive outcome which closely resembles the original manuscript in appearance though not texture. The reprographer has told me his newest photographic equipment can actually enhance the legibility of texts; I certainly find myself handling the printed images with almost as much reverence as I would the originals!